Love's True Home

Love's True Home

Hundreds of original, inspirational quotes, prose, poetry and humor from Facebook's Mystic of Mayhem that will energize your mind, tickle your heart and give each day a loving kick-start.

SRI GAWN TU FAHR

Library of Congress Control Number: 2010910997
ISBN: Hardcover   978-1-4535-4603-1
                 Softcover   978-1-4535-4602-4
                 Ebook   978-1-4535-4604-8

This book was printed in the United States of America.

Sri Gawn Tu Fahr can be found on the World Wide Web @ www.lovestruehome.com, on Facebook and Twitter

Cover art by Dee Laura Sprague (find her on Facebook)

To order additional copies of this book, contact:
Xlibris Corporation
1-888-795-4274
www.Xlibris.com
Orders@Xlibris.com
82644

Contents

Dedication

Love's True Home is dedicated to Oprah Winfrey, a truly inspired soul through whom spirit's love flows into our world like a glorious river of light, and an ecstatic song of joy.

Introduction

May each and every one of you behold and celebrate your true spiritual nature as soul and recognize it in others. We are tears of joy born in the eyes of God. Together, we form a magnificent river of divine love, pulsing in and out of the heart of life.

I didn't set out to write *Love's True Home*. I slowly became aware that it was writing me, so I surrendered and became the Spirit's pen. Love is a gift from God that we share with others, so I share my book with you.

Human experience sparkles with the effervescent sweetness of Spirit's holy breath. *Love's True Home* is a collection of short stories inspired by my interactions with people like you. Each quote is a sparkling comet of love intended to enliven your mind, warm your heart, tickle your belly, and give each day a loving kick-start.

I suggest flipping through these pages and reading the passages at random; let intuition be your guide. Keep *Love's True Home* by your side, and reach for it anytime you experience a bout of spiritual heartburn.

Beholding our true resplendent self for the first time is an exhilarating experience: it's like watching a phoenix rising from the ashes. May the words in these pages rekindle Spirit's sacred flame glowing in your precious heart, love's true home.

You're the best at being you that I have ever seen: so kiss yourself right on the lips, you gorgeous human being.

Chapter 1

Inspiration

I woke up this morning with a sparkle in my eyes; I inhaled love's sweet atoms and drank your warm skies.

Whenever I'm near you my atoms rise and undulate like windblown waves upon a moonlit lake.

A loving heart can never be overfilled; it flows like a resplendent waterfall into the hearts of others. For those who are willing, it just keeps on filling.

You astound me, the way you wrap yourself around me. I love the way you fill me up, and when you drink me up, I can taste your light and feel your sound inside me.

Inspiration is a magic elevator in your heart. What floor are you on? Or have you already blown the roof off your mind and set yourself free?

Intuition is allowing spirit, the voice of God, to be our guide. It beckons from beyond the mind, bringing bounty, joy, and opportunity into our lives. Intuition offers creative solutions to our problems. Open the petals of your inimitable heart, sweet soul, and accept God's gracious love.

> Spread your wings and fly so high,
> Straight through the sun into a brand-new sky,
> You've gotta open up and let it go,
> Open up your heart, and let the good love flow.

It is a very good thing to have abilities in your faith. Why not kick it up a notch and have faith in your abilities? Get off your divine butt, and start spreading the love.

Generosity is an open faucet, a resplendent waterfall, a torrential river and an endless ocean; it is all these things and more.

The creative energy of spirit uses human beings to express itself through various art forms. You are a living, breathing canvas for spirit's light and sound, which can inspire and uplift others. Use your glorious heart to paint life with broad, sweeping brush-strokes of warm love.

I didn't set out to write a book. Gradually, I became aware that it was writing me. I surrendered and became Spirit's pen.

An inspired soul is one through which spirit's love flows like a glorious river of light and an ecstatic song of joy. The sublime sweetness of spirit's holy breath always brightens and enriches the lives of others.

You're the drum in my heart, beating so strong; I'm spirit's sweet echo, singing your song.

You spin madly like a cyclone across my wild terrain, stirring love deep in my heart and wiping out my brain.

I didn't realize I was sleeping until I woke up (to the truth).

Life is for living, and love is for giving, so give it all you've got.

Forget your shortcomings and hug your long-goings.

I love flying in your wondrous sky. I didn't realize I could get so high.

I am a tiger, a wolf, a hawk, and a dove as I explore your worlds of chameleon love.

Did you know that you can flow like a river and fly like the wind and that spirit's sweet love lies waiting within?

Sometimes you are a rain-filled cloud, then suddenly an ocean, and then you whisper like a brook and stir up my emotion.

Each life is a footstep; a lifetime of experience followed by another. Just because you wallowed in mud yesterday doesn't mean you can't ride a comet across the sky today.

Many people have asked me how I come up with so many sayings. The fact of the matter is that the sayings come up with me.

I am a crazy little cyclone spinning 'round your heart, drenching you with golden droplets of liquid love.

When words of love pour from my pen, I know they are not mine; it's Spirit's breath I share with thee, God's precious love sublime.

Trigger-happy, eh? Are you shooting from the dark side or the light side, the outside or the inside? Imagine your heart as a beacon of love, lighting the worlds and the skies up above.

In a dream, I beheld an enormous roaring river pouring from the glorious heavens above to countless worlds below. A cornucopia of celestial sounds issued from this great river, and I realized that this was the fabled sound current, the very foundation upon which all life is created and sustained.

I love to slap the mind around and poke it in the eye, a swift hard kick between the thoughts, and my heart starts to fly.

Leap upon your fast winged horse, O noble rainbow warrior of love. With a smile upon your breast and lightning bolt in hand, you disperse all doubt and darkness and reveal the promised land.

Fill me up, drink me up, and lift me up to the God worlds of divine love.

Load my love into your sacred slingshot, Great Spirit. Shoot me far and deep into the glorious heart of life.

A grain of sand am I upon your beach of love; your gentle breath doth lift me up to God's true home above.

Why waste your life chasing dreams? Set yourself free, and let them catch you.

I am a grateful chalice accepting spirit's endless stream of light and sound. Spirit is the giver, and I am the river through which love flows.

I have completely overdosed from a massive injection of divine love. There is no known cure, and fortunately, it's highly contagious.

As I soar the deep blue skies of your incomparable eyes, the shimmering love light from your heart uplifts and purifies me.

Upon inner reflection, I reach a love connection intersection, which sends me to your sweet perfection.

Only God is God. We exist because of God's love and we are all God's children. Love is a gift from God, which we share with others. Round and round and round it goes, this is how God's sweet love flows.

I don't know how many lifetimes it has taken me to reach this point. Lately, inspiration moves through me like a golden arrow as I behold the sweet sound and light of love in each of your beautiful hearts. Your brilliance gives me wings and sets me free.

I am your kite without a string, and you are my everything.

Imagine yourself swimming effortlessly in an infinite ocean of divine love. You frolic on its gentle waves and then dive into the depths of its inimitable splendor. I see you there smiling; shimmering pearls of liquid love cascading down your blessed body.

> Have you ever stopped to look around and wonder why things are or gazed into the cobalt sky at a distant shining star?
> Have you ever stopped to listen to love's permeating sound, the celestial music of the spheres that all the saints have found?

Sweet love, skip my heart across the ocean like a stone. I'm coming home!

There's no point in being a bird if you don't spread your wings and fly.

Love is always beautiful. Gaze into the mirror and see for yourself.

Occasionally, rivulets of divine inspiration drip out of my consciousness and trickle into my heart. At other times, spirit's love rushes forth like a mighty river and tears asunder the confines of my mind.

> Blue waves a-rollin',
> Gentle breeze in the air,
> Sparkling eyes of little children,
> Love is everywhere.

We are all composed of the same spiritual atoms, but as individual children of God, we express ourselves uniquely. Ka-boom! A supernova of divine love bursts from our hearts.

Life is for living, and love is for giving, so give it all you've got.

Unleash your power, love and wisdom; allow the brilliance of your golden heart to show you the way.

Why flicker like a flame when a roaring fire burns inside?

Spirit knows what is best for us. Divine inspiration comes in many styles, fashions, degrees, aromas, colors, etc. By relaxing, we allow spirit to work through us. Learn to recognize the nudges, opportunities, and wonderful gifts awaiting us at every turn.

The higher I fly, the deeper I get.

Some of you are looking for the source of life. Did you know that it is looking for you?

Sometimes I think like Eckhart Tolle, and then I feel like Rumi; sometimes there's Einstein in my wine as Dr. Seuss flows through me.

Spirit speaks to those whose eyes and ears are open. It might be the look in a stranger's eyes, a friend, a child's smile, a passage from a book, a movie, our pets, music, dreams or a loving embrace. Look, listen, and be grateful for spirit's love.

Hand in hand we walk along the shores of life. Whitecaps foam and whisper tales, then disappear again.

In a dream, I walked naked through a shimmering valley, high in the sacred mountains of a distant world. The air was warm and moist; the ice I trod upon sparkled like precious jewels. As I neared the precipice, I became intoxicated with joy. Suspended high above me in a liquid azure sky, three golden suns drenched my perfect body with benevolent rays of pure liquid love.

> How high is high?
> How deep is deep?
> How far is far?
> Dare you peep?
> How long before you rise above
> into the worlds of God's sweet love?

Your joy is my joy is our joy is spirit's joy is love's joy.

Thou art the sun, the prism, and the rainbow. Thou art soul, child of God, perfect and free.

If you love to write, draw, paint, teach, or any other creative endeavor, chances are you excel at it. When we love to do something, we do it well because it comes from the heart. Make time in your busy life to do what you love; everyone benefits, including you. Allow the sweetness and splendor of your inimitable love to shine from within.

Tears of joy flow like a mighty river from my heart whenever I behold your brilliant countenance.

Thou art the candle, and I am the flame. I burn forever in thy name.

> Life: like skies full of rain, pours down in torrents, and then rises again.
> Death: like trees in the fall, bare all their branches 'til they hear the spring call.
> Cycles: what appears to be starting has recently waned, and what seems to be passing is sprouting again.

If you want to build up a great credit rating in the spiritual world, simply pull out your Master-charge; use it often to fly the friendly skies within your golden heart.

You are never alone. Gaze into the brilliant splendor of your incomparable heart. You are freedom, love, power, and wisdom. No one—including all spiritual teachers, guides, and masters—can give you what you already have. Love is all there is.

I am a feather floating upon the waves of God's lovely laughter. Cradle me in your arms, sweet spirit, and carry me into the bosom of your heart.

I am not here to serve humankind. I serve only God. Spirit's love flows from my heart and sees to it that humankind is well served.

Your imagination is a most wonderful gift, so use it in a positive, creative manner. Perhaps you imagine that your heart has wheels, sails, or even wings. However you see it, know that your heart can set you free. As soul, you are a divine instrument through which the love of God flows. Imagine that, eh?

If you truly look for goodness in every heart you meet, joy will greet you every time with a tender kiss so sweet.

> You arrived on the breath of a wind
> and sparked my fire within.
> That's when my life began
> on the road to understanding love.

There's no limit on dreams, and your heart is boundless, so what the heck are you waiting for?

I feel like Rumi on a rocket as I zoom across the heavens with your warm heart in my pocket.

A person whom a dimwit considers to be brilliant is nothing more than a slightly brighter dimwit.

> Some people love to get off,
> and some love to get it on.
> Some love to get on with it,
> and some just don't get it.
> Some prefer the get-go,
> and some just gotta go.
> Some like to get it over with,
> and some like to go get it.
> I decided to forget it
> and let it all go
> and I have never regretted it.

Imagination creates worlds of unlimited possibilities. Lack of imagination creates worlds of unlimited impossibilities.

I am not a person who likes to still my mind by concentrating and passively withdrawing from the outer world. I prefer to play with the endless streams of thought as they flow through my consciousness. I marvel as they reveal a cornucopia of divine possibilities. This active world of contemplation is my source of inspiration.

> I love being chased by my dreams
> as I frolic here and scamper there.
> Come on little dream; catch me if you dare.

Listen to the sound of the river. I've got something to give her deep in my heart.

I enjoy being a beach on the shoreline of your love. Your warm iridescent waters beckon me with each wave as you pull me from the sand. I'm a sandman flowing through your hands.

The light of you is all I see; with darkness gone, now I am free.

I am feeling so humongous right now that I can barely contain myself.

Are you trying to push something over? Try uprooting it instead.

> Wrap your loving tendrils gently 'round my heart and hug me warm and deep,
> Wake me from this ancient slumber; lift me from my sleep.

I didn't realize how special life was until you opened my heart.

Ladders are useful devices for those who have yet to discover their wings.

The only thing I don't like about being a child is that everybody wants me to grow up.

Whenever I behold thy brilliant countenance, I am a heavenly feather filled with joy as I ride the sacred wind within your precious heart.

If you want to see something truly spectacular, replace everything with nothing, and all shall be revealed.

When you live your life fully from the heart, your mind can't come inside; the light and sound of spirit's breath vanquishes all pride.

"Humblifted"—a state in which I am humbled and uplifted by the gentle grace of a loving soul.

My mind's a machine, my heart's electricity; when you push my love button, we become synchronicity.

Chapter 2

Why God Laughs

I'm tired of having to take responsibility for my actions. Is anyone in the mood for taking on a little blame?

Logic definitely has its place. I keep mine gagged and tightly bound in the garage.

Mind without a heart is like gas without a fart. The pressure keeps building, and there's no relief in sight.

> I don't know what it is about you, mind.
> Sometimes you're quite obscene.
> As I bathe in love's sweet nectar,
> you toss pickles in my cream.

Holy horse plop! I just realized that I have spent my entire life getting to where I am right now! What a trip!

When it comes to duality, there are two sides to every story.

Saints are not immune to the wide spectrum of human ailments. I am presently writing a short story about a great soul, a pilgrim of peace who suffered from frequent bouts of flatulence. He transformed this curse into a benefit by using it to propel himself across an entire country on a cloud of methane. It's been a real gas writing it. The working title is "Gandhi with the Wind."

Whew! That was close. I almost got there before I arrived!

Recently, someone called me an 'a-hole.' Feeling rather smug, I replied that I was well versed in the entire alphabet of lurid possibilities and considered myself to be a well-rounded 'a-to-z-hole.'

When I was a kid, adults would ask me, "What are you going to be when you grow up?" I told them that I never gave it much thought because I already knew who I was.

The only problem with being here now is that I'm always somewhere else when I'm thinking about it.

Being hung up on the past is like looking over your shoulder and staring at your ass. You can't see where you're going, and no matter how long you stare at it, it'll never be what it's "cracked up" to be. What a bummer, eh?

I was feeling so low when I woke up this morning that I had to climb an eighteen-foot extension ladder to get up to the basement, but I'm all right now.

Where there's a will, there's a way, while a horde of lawyers and greedy relatives fidget, bicker, and drool on the sidelines.

Life could be likened to a sandwich. Everyone wants a bite, but not everybody wants to share. Chomp!

My dad used to say, "It's the little things in life that count, so use your head."

This is the first time in my life I have ever made a resolution and stuck to it. On New Year's eve, I vowed that I would live 'til the day I died. So far, it's going pretty darn good.

Whoever invented the phrase "I'm bored" probably had nothing better to do.

Timing can be quite important. Next time you embark on a journey of any kind—be it physical, mental, emotional, or spiritual—try your very best to get there at exactly the same time as you arrive. You'll be amazed by the results.

I welcome your opinion as long as you don't make any suggestions.

Yesterday, I was sitting at a local cafe slurping back a cup of coffee when a stranger approached my table and asked, "Can I join you?" I quickly scanned my body from top to bottom and replied, "Why, am I coming apart?"

Jeeeeez! If this keeps up, it will never come down.

Life could be likened to a cow. It always seems greener on the udder side, with a never-ending stream of bull to contend with.

As I stood at the edge of the precipice, my nose began to tingle wildly as fluorescent sparks shot out of my nostrils. Suddenly, I left my body; hovering above the time track, I witnessed past, present and future events simultaneously. All of creation lay before me; everything made scents to my holy proboscis, a true beak-on of truth. Henceforth, I became known as Nostrildamus, he who nose all.

Such joy I experienced this morning when I woke up and discovered that I still had a pulse.

Not long ago, I was so underwhelmed by a lack of anything significant in my life that I totally collapsed under the sheer weightlessness of my immeasurable nothingness.

Our local college is offering an excellent course on memory enhancement, but I keep forgetting to go.

What a shock it was to observe my gentle-natured vegetarian friend as he unleashed a flurry of violence today. I watched in horror as he poked the potatoes in the eyes, yanked the corn by the ears, squeezed a head of lettuce, and cut the heart out of an artichoke.

A recent survey suggests that pregnancy is a leading cause of childbirth.

I would rather be a moron than a moroff. I speak from experience.

Who invented this planet, anyway? I would like to know because they included me without my permission. I want off immediately, please.

When I was a young boy, my dad told me that he would teach me to be gentle, peaceful, and loving; even if it meant that he had to beat it into me.

I went for a visit to our local acupuncturist this morning, and he gave me a few good "pointers." Spirit speaks in mysterious ways.

Silence is a topic that is exceedingly difficult to discuss.

It is hilarious that some who claim that they can predict the future and others who say that they can see into the past don't even have a clue what's going on right now.

I didn't realize what all the laughter was about until I looked in the mirror.

Attempting to build an entire city with only a hammer in hand is no more ridiculous than using the mind to understand love. Boot! Whoops! Sorry, Mr. Mind. I didn't mean to kick you between the thoughts.

I knew something was slightly awry this morning when I woke up and found myself singing "You Make Me Feel Like a Natural Woman."

My former psychic was shocked and surprised when I dropped in unexpectedly.

After studying polygamy for several years, I came to the conclusion that there are too many sides to consider.

Someone told me I was responsible for the earthquake, that it was my fault. I tried to blame it on San Andreas.

Many people believe they are what they eat. I prefer to eat what I am.

I am in a very fowl mood because someone just stapled a chicken to my forehead.

Never ask a liar why he or she is lying. It's like asking a selfish tear why the heck it's always crying.

Whenever I get all tanked up on love's sweet juice, I get to feeling like I'm Doctor Seuss, a rogue on the loose chasing Mother Goose. As I ride spirit's train, I'm a crazy caboose with a one-track mind; and your succulent heart, I seek to find.

I wasn't reading your mind. It was reading me.

It is so quiet in here that I can hear a mouse peeing on a Kleenex.

The largest thing I have ever seen turned out to be much smaller than I expected.

Guess what? I saved $250,000 today. I didn't buy a Ferrari.

Today, I am enjoying being around. Yesterday, I enjoyed being a cube, and the day before, I had a wonderful time being a pyramid. Variety is the spice of my life, and your star-filled eyes and iridescent smile are my inspiration.

Not long ago, I was laughing so hard at myself that my mask dropped off. I was shocked! Until that moment, I didn't know I was wearing one. I scurried to the nearest mirror to see what I looked like. Much to my surprise, I was still wearing sunglasses. Making a spectacle of myself once again. Does it ever end?

Human beings are living proof that God has an incredible sense of humor.

Last night, I had a dream in which I couldn't remember who I was. When I woke up this morning, I realized that I don't even know who I am.

For some strange reason, I find myself striving for the same goal every single day: trying to go out of my mind and get into my heart. Jeez! Will it ever end?

The ego is wrapped up with itself in constant adulation: a frantic, self-indulgent, repugnant mindsturbation.

A control freak is actually a controlled freak under the crushing thumb of the mechanical mind.

One of the most embarrassing moments in my life was when the cops pulled over and charged me with impersonating a human.

I like the saying "live and learn." If I were a batter in major leagues baseball, I'd be a living legend, batting 500. One out of two isn't bad; at least I'm living.

My insanity is the only thing preventing me from losing my mind!

The only thing I don't like about spontaneity is that it always shows up unexpectedly.

The fact that greed can be shared is an oxymoron of immense proportions.

Have you heard about the upcoming International Hermit Convention? I wonder if anyone will show up?

Infants are the root cause of all senior citizens.

Chapter 3

Problem Solving

Got egg on your face? Feeling disgraced? No worries. Perk up your smile, light up your eyes, and fling omelets of love high into the skies.

If it weren't for challenges, human beings wouldn't exist.

The farther we can see, the less we have to look. Eventually, we stop searching and see it all.

We are never presented with problems too large to solve. All answers lie within. The fact that we can perceive a problem is proof that we can solve it.

I think the main reason I am so good at making mistakes is because I get plenty of practice. I constantly strive to improve my failures and aim to single-handedly dig the world's deepest hole. Life is a riot!

Are you feeling burdened by the weight of life's hardships? Allow Spirit's sweet breath to fill the sails of your heart ship.

Recognizing a problem is a good start; complaining about it accomplishes nothing. If we want the world to change, we have to change. Spiritual growth is an individual endeavor, not a group mentality.

> The harder you look, the less you will find.
> Trust in your heart, and abandon the mind.
> Set yourself free and be who you are:
> perfect, eternal, inimitable star.

I prefer to start at the top and work my way down. This approach gives me a bigger picture, a better overview of the smaller pieces, which comprise the whole.

The magnitude of our so-called problems and challenges are directly proportionate to the degree in which love is lacking in our life.

Many of my friends have asked me if I am always in a good space, seeing love everywhere with a smile forever on my face? The answer is no; it just isn't so. I average about 1,000 negative thoughts a day, but spirit's sweet love shines from your heart and washes them all away.

Problems and personal challenges are never-ending. As long as we are experiencing new ones, we know we are growing.

Here is a neat little trick I employ when confronted by people who are trying to piss me off, criticize me, etc: instead of reacting to them negatively, which keeps me connected to them, I become a mirror and let the energy reflect back to them, maintaining my dignity all the while. I call it organic human pest control.

Instead of trying to learn a new trick or skill, let it learn you. Make room for it by expanding your consciousness, and allow it to grow.

Love teaches us difficult lessons sometimes. Spirit is always seeking finely tuned souls to use as beacons to shine its love light.

A mistake is an opportunity to learn a lesson and grow in a certain area. Problems and challenges are never ending. They exist to temper us and prepare us for greater things.

Failure can be a very important step toward achieving success.

"The bigger the challenge, the greater opportunity for growth" means that we should be very grateful for the challenges in our life, for without problems, there would be no solutions and no spiritual advancement.

Things, which can't be proven by the logical mind, are truths far beyond space and time.

When someone attempts to insult me, it is like throwing splinters at the sun. Their pointed barbs vaporize long before they reach their intended target.

There isn't a problem or challenge that can't be solved. In this world of duality, everything has its opposite: male/female, up/down, hot/cold, etc. The opposite of a problem is a solution. Whenever you perceive a problem, try to remember that every answer resides within your loving heart.

Only humans "try" to live and love. Microorganisms, plants, and animals mastered it billions of years ago.

The expressions "never give up" and "don't give up" are strange. I have discovered that the more love I do give up, the more adventurous and fulfilling my life becomes. I do my best to "give up" as much love as I can.

If you pull yourself back far enough from anything, the details disappear and you can see the whole thing, the big picture. When you zoom back in, the details make a lot more sense. How far can you pull back? How big is your picture?

Instead of trying to overcome something, why not undercome it, thereby saving a lot of valuable time (which doesn't exist anyway)?

Do you find yourself saying "I can't take it any longer?" Well, simply stop "taking" it. Let it go, release it, and stop fighting. Behold the love within your heart, and start "giving" it.

The only problem with the mind is that it exists.

If the same problem keeps reappearing, it means we need to apply ourselves diligently in that area of our life. We learn from our experiences sooner or later.

I no longer face my fears. They were blinded by your love and fell into arrears.

> The more you try to do,
> the less you will get done;
> so open up your precious heart,
> and share with everyone.

Whenever you try to push someone's buttons, you are allowing the mind to push yours.

Being lighthearted is a key to happiness. When we look "out there" and see life's problems, we don't have to take them seriously or let them bother us. We can say, "I didn't create that, so I'm not going to take responsibility for it. I take responsibility for my own actions." If everyone lived his or her life in this manner, more love would flow throughout the land.

Spiritual truths are so simple that most people overlook them, which is exactly what the mind wants.

Why face your fears? Simply do an about-face, and embrace your love.

Did someone throw tomatoes in your face today? Don't let it get you down! Get creative, and make tomato sauce tomorrow.

Sometimes it is better to walk around a problem instead of headfirst into it. Not all of them need to be solved. We decide which ones offer the greatest potential benefits for our spiritual growth.

Chapter 4

Divinity of Woman

When I say I love you, I am reflecting what I see, feel, hear, touch, and taste. The sweet nectar lies within thee, precious woman, and flows like a majestic waterfall from your heart into mine.

The divinity of a woman affects me like an exquisite painting. I stand there mesmerized by her beauty, splendor, and mystery as I am drawn deep into her heart. O sweet woman, God's greatest gift to man.

I'm the crust, and you are the topping; your hot, tangy sauce has my love atoms popping!

In the heart of every woman glows a precious perfect jewel, delicious and delightful; it brightens every fool. She's the key to liberation for every breathing man, so dive into her splendor, and love her while you can.

Wrap yourself around me, woman, until my love erupts; a honeybee my heart is now, and you, my buttercup.

> I know you think you can't be caught,
> but I'm on the hunt for what you've got.
> Your scents so strong, and you're scorching hot,
> so I've hatched up a real good plot.
> I've laid a trap that you can't see;
> I'll jump your flame and set you free.
> I'll set up camp and pitch my tent
> and love you to your heart's content.

Woman, you are my heart's only desire, and transform my flame into a roaring fire.

Beauty, proportion, balance, grace, symmetry, harmony, and wonder: all this and more I taste, touch, smell, see, hear and feel in thee, sweet woman of mystery.

> We whirl around each other,
> as sparks fly everywhere
> Colliding with such tenderness,
> there's nothing to compare.

I'm a fiery comet of love inviting you along for a ride. Hop on my wings, and hold on tight as I fly straight into your heart and emerge as a glorious sunrise in the tropical skies of your deep smoldering eyes.

Ka-boom! A billion volts of lightning love illuminate the sky. Toss your heart up to me, babe; together, we shall fly.

I find it easy to communicate with women. I behold, acknowledge, and express my sincere appreciation for their majestic beauty, poetic grace, and sweet sublime mystery.

The sweet perfume of thy simmering love permeates the innermost chamber of my grateful heart. You truly are heaven's scent.

I love intermingling with you; our heart song, a love jingle as our senses tingle from the invigorating warmth of spirit's holy breath.

> You're a mad, sexy, precocious yin,
> an enticing psychotropic spin.
> I'm a crazy catalytic yang,
> a supernova rainbow twang.
> We twist and shout and scream and fly,
> then dive into each other eyes.

I love spinning with you around this flame. Enough of this earthly game! Let's aim high for the heavens in our hearts. Spirit's love beckons.

A woman is not something to figure out, understand, or analyze. Forget the musing of the mind; immerse yourself deep in her eyes.

I can feel your love all over. I shudder as it moves through me, throughout me, with me, and without me.

The love in your eyes makes a lot of scents, and my grateful heart inhales them all.

Whenever you giggle, tiny love bubbles burst out of your heart and sprinkle upon me like golden rain-shine. How I love thee, sweet woman.

I can taste your juicy pheromones as they wander through my mist. They land upon my love-filled heart with a luscious holy kiss.

Whoops! I didn't intend to swallow you whole, but you looked so scrumptious that I succumbed to a torrid love frenzy and lost all control.

Can you feel the thunder as my passion tears your heart asunder? Let it go, don't hang on; my love's the sun in your new dawn.

Although we are both aware that I turned you on, I also realize that you reserve the right to turn me off at any given moment.

My tears of joy are transformed into glittering emeralds when they alight upon your love-filled heart.

I'm frantically searching your heart for a thermostat 'cause your heat's too phat, and it's knocked me down flat.

I surrender and free-fall heart first into the gleaming galaxies deep within your smoldering eyes.

Sweet nectar rushes from your golden heart like a mighty roaring river and washes over me. Thou art heavenly ambrosia, sweet woman, forever quenching my thirst.

My precious woman! As we wrap ourselves around each other, our atoms intermingle in an effervescent dance of joy! Together, we form a shimmering double helix of golden love, giving birth to countless new constellations. How I love thee!

I love to fly so high with you, hand in hand, our wing tips igniting—your light so exciting. I dive into your eyes, deep oceans of warm liquid love. I love to fly so high with you.

Whenever I gaze upon thy beautiful countenance, my entire being rejoices, my senses scintillating with brightness so intense that I shoot out from the center of my heart high up into the sky, and then dive like a golden eagle straight into yours. My lover, perfect soul, child of God; I bathe in the waters of your inimitable splendor forever.

Sweet woman! Thou art a precious jewel in love's bright crown. Your kiss spins my heart 'round and 'round; I never ever want to come down.

> I love to take my starlit brush and run it through
> your hair,
> Gazing deep within your eyes, I kiss your skin
> so fair.
> In thee I love to swim and glide,
> your pleasures so divine.
> Heaven's home, I've found at last,
> your heart is Rumi's rhyme.

I know it is unethical—theft is not allowed. But I just want to steal your heart 'cause it melts away my shroud.

Woman! What is it about your love that sends my heart shooting up to the stars? I am singing your name.

I am the waves beneath your boat; upon my love your heart does float.

O precious woman, my heart is a chalice, and thou art the wine. Pour thyself into me, sweet love sublime.

Your precious tender loving eyes mesmerize, tantalize, and lift me up to golden skies.

I love to feast on the fruit of your intense desire. Your sweetness washes over me as I explore the mysteries in your loving heart.

I love taking a bubble bath in the fountain of your heart.

I am a solitary tiger roaming the sultry tropical forest of your heart. I never tire on my journey as I draw ever closer to the fountain of your love.

The sweetest of all my dreams came true the first time I set my eyes on you.

All I can say about pleasure and joy is I'm glad you're a girl and thank God I'm a boy.

> What makes a woman a woman
> and a man a man
> aside from the juices
> that pulse in their glands?
> What is this yin, and what is this yang?
> Theories abound with a clamorous clang!
> Here's what I've learned,
> and here's what I share,

when I'm entwined with you, darling,
I no longer care.

I love being inside you, moving slowly as I ride the rhythmic undulations of your love until I tumble over spirit's waterfall and splash into your heart.

Your sweet moonbeams elevate my dreams to places I have never been. I love thee, precious woman.

Ahhh! Once again, your majestic heavenly eyes and sweet loving voice are working their charming spell. Off I go on an enchanting magic carpet ride, the very fabric of this carpet woven from the spiritual fibers of your love-filled heart.

The closest I can get to pure physical joy and pleasure in this world is when I am entwined with my lover's body, inseparable, as one: loving, intermingling, and sharing with each other unconditionally. The beauty, grace, sweet delight, and sublime mystery of a woman, God's greatest gift to man.

> My heart is a-blazin'
> and my mind is awhirl,
> I'm gonna tickle your fancy
> and polish your pearl.
> Nothing can stop me,
> I've gotta have you, girl.

How lovely it is to drown in your waters and be reborn as a wave of liquid love dancing upon the surface of your golden heart.

I am so obsessed with you, precious woman. Love pours from your heart and washes over me. Thy glory sets me free.

I love the way our atoms collide, merging and dancing so deep inside with nothing to hide as our hearts open wide. I love the way our atoms collide.

Each beat of your glowing heart gives birth to countless brilliant constellations. Your glorious love light shatters my mind into a million fragments, and I am reborn as an angelic wave upon your inimitable ocean of love and splendor. With wings in my heart, I fly forever in your eyes.

I'm standing at the plate and waiting for the throw. Toss your heart straight at me, babe, it's the only way to go.

Whenever I say I love you completely, I am truly out of my mind.

I feel like a "wrap" artist as I prepare my gifts of gratitude for your precious heart.

My favorite color is the rainbow in your loving heart.

I am a troubadour sitting upon the window ledge of your heart. My song of love cries to enter thy heavenly paradise. Sweet woman, I am yours forever and a day.

I don't think I could possibly love you more. I know I can always love you better.

I'm dipping my ladle of love into the waters of your precious heart. The taste of you sends me reeling.

I love to tickle your heart because whenever you laugh, your love splashes back; sweet droplets of heavenly nectar bathing me in you.

I find myself waking up in a dream to a spectacular sunrise on the soft, sandy shores of your pristine heart. I have my trusty little canoe with me and am eager to venture forth and explore the mystic waters deep within your love.

Luscious love drips from your lips and seeps into my heart. It stirs an ancient longing and blows my mind apart.

I don't like being around explosives, but whenever I'm near you, your scorching beauty and intoxicating aroma blows my mind to smithereens and makes my heart pop like a cosmic lollipop.

I'm joyful when our atoms merge into a loving molecule, the way our passion clusters; I think it's really kewl.

You love to ping, and I love to pong; I can play this game all life long.

I am a little honeybee laden with pollen; I can taste your sweet nectar. I can hear your heart callin'.

I am a flame reaching higher and higher as I breathe in the heat of your intense desire. I didn't think I could get any higher until my heart dove into the depths of your fire.

> I love this sea of women,
> each wave a magic dance,
> I surf their holy waters
> and upon each one I prance.
> My heart soars like a comet
> as I scream my song of joy,
> I thank the Holy Spirit
> for making me a boy.

Your sweetness shines upon me, endearing
and so bright.
I'm your knight in shining armor, reflecting
your love light.
Climb upon my holy steed, and together, we
shall roam
across the skies in spirit's eyes to God's eternal
home.

Myriad wonders and mysteries thou art, precious woman; so many ways to see, taste, feel, think, and imagine you. I immerse myself deep within thee and bathe forever in the resplendent crystalline waters of your golden heart.

I didn't realize that I was lost until you found me, sweet woman.

Many women are saddened by the fact that men don't come with warranties or instruction manuals. What woman wants to riffle through five hundred pages just to see how the darn thing works? I'm glad that women don't come with a how-to book. I'm a hands-on kind of guy: always eager to explore, learn, and share.

Precious jewel art thou, sweet lady. Every blessed facet of your exquisite being enthralls me. The splendor of your love light elevates me far beyond the heavens above. As I gaze upon thee, a river of love erupts from my heart and flows joyfully into yours. I am truly free within thee.

You are the herbs, and I am the spices; our loving concoction dissolves all our vices.

Your heart is heaven's apple; the taste of you is exquisite, divine, and uplifting.

Your heart is a symphony of light and sound. I'm spinning round and round and never ever coming down.

In my heart, I have a tummy; and when you dive in, it whispers, "Yummy."

Hey, darlin', got a light? No, not that! I'm sure there's one glowing in your heart because you're so smoking hawt!

Forget the so-called G-spot. When I'm with my lover, I sample every luscious letter of the alphabet and throw in a few of my own spicy characters for extra body and flavor.

The brightest of all constellations pales compared to your love light, sweet woman. Your sweetness sends me to places that don't exist.

In a dream, I awoke, realizing we had been here many times before. My lover and I hovered above a luminescent babbling brook, mesmerized, as it whispered sublime secrets. Suddenly, a legion of angels erupted from our radiant hearts, and the brook became a heavenly waterfall of liquid emeralds bathing us with spirit's heavenly nectar.

I love to kiss your tender skin; my heart melts when you let me in.

How wonderful it is to watch you sleep, and then awaken in my own dream, entwined around your body as we make love in one of God's glorious mystical paintings.

I'm a tyrannosaur of love like you've never seen, I'm gonna take you places where you've never been.

I love it when we wrap ourselves around each other.

The mind of man is all wrapped up in thinking and deduction. The heart of woman pulses strong with mystery and seduction.

You are the every woman that every man dreams of loving.

As I reach up to the heavens and spread my arms, a flock of shimmering alabaster doves bursts from my heart, carrying your message of love to the four corners of all creation. How I love thee, sweet spirit.

> If I became you and you became me,
> Would we be each other?
> Would we be together?
> Would we be as one?
> Would we have one heart?
> Would we have some fun?

Entering a woman's heart is like waking up in a remote mountain valley enlivened with the scintillating scent of spring's fresh breath: wildflowers in resplendent bloom with the sun shining high above, pouring down buckets of sweet liquid love.

You and I are the perfect loving equation.

> Your heart is all shiny, sparkling and bright
> Your eyes, constellations bringing joy to the night
> Your smiles, streaming comets; your hair, liquid fire
> Woman, thou truly are my heart's one desire.

Chapter 5

Obedietrons

In the lower worlds, we often forget our true nature as soul and become subject to the influence of those who try to control us through the use of fear and intimidation. Believing that we are a body, emotions or our thoughts make us easy prey. Behold your true radiant self, and set yourself free.

Most of what I've been taught by others isn't worth knowing. The true gems lie waiting within myself.

A symbol might seem awesome at first until you realize that it stands between you and the real thing.

Sometimes it feels like I'm in a prison but not a typical prison in which I am being held against my will: I am the warden here. The mind enthralls me with all the trappings of the outer world, and I indulge in greed. At other times, love fills my heart, and the prison walls dissipate like fog melting in the midday sun.

The intellectual concept of a messiah is presented by the mind as a promise, causing many to look toward the future, hoping for some kind of salvation. Love, power, wisdom, and freedom exist in the ever-present moment of the now. The messiah as a poetic symbol points to divine love residing in our hearts, love's true home. Look no further! You are the messiah.

Life on planet Earth is a game with preset rules. The pesky mind chooses to ignore these rules and spews a relentless cacophony of pathetic human rules with a singular goal: to control us and mold us into robotic obedietrons. When I gaze into my shimmering golden heart, I see the higher law of divine love, the key to spiritual freedom.

We don't really have a mind; more often than not, mind has us in its grip. We can choose to remain in this worldly prison and fight for freedom, justice, and equality from within its walls or rise above it and enter into a world of divine love. Look no further than your heart, O precious one.

Imagine billions of beings living in a room so vast that few can see its walls: Every human experience occurs within these confines. This gigantic room is your mind, and until you can get beyond it, you will continue to live within its limitations, all the while believing you are free. Your golden heart is the door to true spiritual freedom.

I just realized why we have an indentation between our shoulder blades. It's from many lifetimes of patting ourselves on the back and congratulating ourselves in recognition of humanity's awesome accomplishments.

Many people pursue goals that others have deemed worthwhile. The only goal worth pursuing is to have no goals whatsoever. Why strive for love when it sits waiting in your heart?

Most of us don't realize we are spiritual travelers with a unique purpose in life. Our purpose has nothing to do with human-made laws, which strive to control us. We are goddesses and gods of our own universe. Embrace the eternal liberating love residing in your heart, and set yourself free.

One of the greatest challenges of the human state of consciousness is that we often find ourselves looking outward at life and reacting to others. This is where blame originates. What we experience in the outer world is a reflection of our inner states. When our hearts are filled with love, we see love all around us.

Spirit is gracious and loving; it doesn't boss us around. We are granted freedom of choice, our spiritual birthright. Only people and organizations bark out orders. Spirit points the way by shining its love light, and we make our own decisions in our search for truth. This is true freedom, which calls for great personal responsibility.

What would it be like if all human rules, laws, regulations, dogmas, and creeds suddenly vanished? Wow! Things are looking great now! Human laws aren't necessary. They exist to control us by telling us what to do, how to live our lives, etc. I do my best to observe the one true law: all souls exist because of God's love.

What many call the comfort zone is actually very uncomfortable. Many choose to put up with the misery rather than go for the gusto, which requires motivation and individual effort to see beyond the norm, disregard the status quo, and transcend the walls of illusions created by the mind. Gaze within, rev up the engine of your glorious heart, and let love be your guide.

In our world, there are different types and varying degrees of relative truths. What is true for one doesn't necessarily apply to another. Morals, customs, traditions, religion, and cultural influences are all factors arising from group consciousness and have nothing to do with what is right or wrong.

A strange world exists in which everyone is born wearing five layers of clothing: physical, emotional, causal, mental, and ethereal. Most only see the physical layer and believe they are a body. A naked man and woman appear and ask, "What's with all the clothes?" For some, this is a revelation; and as they peel away the layers, the sweet love light in their golden hearts begins to shine through.

Chapter 6

Divine Love

May all souls behold and celebrate their true spiritual nature as children of God and recognize it in others. We are tears of joy born in the eyes of God. Together, we form a magnificent river of divine love pulsing in and out of the heart of life.

The manner in which divine inspiration manifests is exquisite. Spirit enters our golden hearts, absorbing our unique color, texture, flavor, and aroma and flows out again as a river of love, uplifting all life through our noble thoughts, loving feelings, and acts of kindness.

Why search for love? It can never be found. It has always existed in God's light and sound.

Although divine truth is constant, the message is always updated and expressed in various manners and forms to suit the consciousness of the times.

The sweetest of all things is love from the heart.

> You appeared to me on a cloud of white,
> Luminous being, O great source of life,
> Words can't describe, and thoughts can't express
> Your haunting beauty and sweet caress.

Once we release the tight grip we have on the temporal objects of this ghostly world, we are free to embrace divine love glowing in our hearts.

I speak to the love in thy radiant heart, O perfect soul.

Divine love has no depth, width, length, or weight: it can't be measured. Cast away your feeble worldly instruments and open up your magnificent heart.

Love is a flower displaying her beauty, illuminating life, and sharing her glory for all to enjoy.

When you are ready, love will find you and shine through the window in your heart.

Every day is a perfect day for love.

Within every single sparkling atom of your spiritual body, there are countless galaxies teeming with divine love.

The human heart and divine heart are not one and the same; in one shines precious love whilst the other harbors pain.

Divine love inhabits the spaces in between the things I see.

God is too pure to contact us directly. It makes itself known to us by way of its sound and light, commonly referred to as spirit. Can you hear it? Can you see it? Can you feel it? I can taste it! Divine love beckons us home as it speaks from our hearts.

No teaching is worth a pinch of mouse poop unless it is imbued with divine love and speaks to the heart.

There is no opposite of divine love, the source of life itself. Some think it is fear or hate, but these indicate an absence of love.

In the eyes of a babe, in the coo of a dove are inscribed the wonders of divine love.

The reason you love the way I write is because I write the way you love.

I am a heavenly faucet pouring spirit's love into the hot tub of life.

My love is like a windshield wiper washing clean your pane.

From divine love is born wisdom, power, and freedom.

Love is the only thing that can never be exhausted.

The thoughts and feelings we choose to harbor in our consciousness become the flora and fauna in the forests and meadows of our hearts.

I joyfully reflect divine love radiating from your precious hearts.

Many strive to acquire what they find lacking in their lives without realizing that everything required for a bountiful existence lies waiting in every heart.

I am blessed with the ability to stand way back, look at the whole picture, and behold the hand of God behind all human activity. I see divine love in every precious human heart.

It is easier to dig a tunnel to the center of the Earth with a toothpick than it is to discover divine love with the mind.

Although our eyes reveal a cornucopia of people, physical things, and events in the world, they have no lasting value. All things must pass; why not gaze at divine love, forever breathing and shining in your golden heart?

True love is a state of being, and true being is a state of loving.

The first time I met you, I spontaneously gave birth to a second heart to catch the glorious river of love pouring from your eyes.

Love by itself won't pay bills, save lives, or end suffering. Spirit doesn't interfere with human activity. It constantly searches for more willing beacons to shine its love light. As more conscious souls accept God's love, the brighter life becomes. Turn yourself on, O love-filled one.

Forget everything that is outside of you. It's not easy, but I can promise you this: love resides within your heart and mine. I give myself completely to you. Give yourself back to me, sweet soul, and realize what it means to be free.

True love is always a win-win situation.

God is not found out there. The experience of God is an inner, personal experience that can't be proven by one person to another. When we move beyond the mind and gaze into our golden hearts, we experience God in a personal manner. All life exists because of God's love. This is all we need to know.

The things in life that are hidden from our physical eyes reveal themselves in their entire splendor when we gaze into our loving hearts.

True love can never be measured. It can only be treasured.

> I can't be lost and can't be found,
> I'm in the air and in the ground;
> I'm very loud without a sound.
> I'm everywhere yet can't be seen,
> I'm where you're going
> and where you've been.
> I never stop and never start;
> I am spirit's love, which fills your heart.

Trying to understand love with the mind is like wearing a suit of armor while sunbathing on an exotic beach; spirit's light can't reach you, and life becomes hot and unbearable. Free yourself from the shackles of the mechanical mind; cast away your mental cloaks and emotional veils. Thou art soul, forever free, a love-filled child of God.

The words luck and lucky exist due to a misunderstanding. What you consider to be lucky is in fact a blessing, a gift from spirit that you have earned. Whenever God's love smiles upon thee, remember to be grateful for your fortune, a gift of love.

Imagine being curious without asking any questions. Whenever we ask a question, we stop and wait for an answer. A curious soul lives in the moment and is always giving because it knows that love is the only answer to which there is no question.

I have nothing to give because I am all yours, sweet spirit.

The wider the space is between my ears, the greater my joy and the fewer my fears.

Now that you've realized that you are a divine seedling, it's time to sprout some wings and flitter joyfully in the light of spirit's love.

Your loving heart isn't something you walk into or meet along the way. It is where you live, love, and shine every single day.

A relationship without trust is like a flower without water and sunshine; it can never blossom forth in all the ways it was intended. Open up the petals of your inimitable heart, and soak in the nourishing rays of God's divine love light.

Third dimension? Fourth dimension? Fifth dimension? It doesn't matter; they're all limited constructs of the mechanical mind, trapped forever in matter and time. Love has no dimensions; stop measuring, and start treasuring.

The ultimate sacrifice for a human being is to give up one's own life so that another may live.

Love is the prime creative force. How well we work with it determines the nature and quality of our experiences.

Chapter 7

Science—That's Entertainment

Science claims that we utilize about 10 percent of our brainpower. Yikes! What a terrifying thought. Imagine what would happen if the remaining 90 percent jumped on the bandwagon. I'm heading for the hills!

It is interesting to note that in today's technologically advanced societies, there isn't a single scientific instrument in existence that can measure love.

Science only measures the "results" or "effects" of matter moving through space. Since all matter eventually disintegrates, science is incapable of knowing anything of lasting value. Let's hear your response to that one, Mr. Mind. Whoops! I apologize. I didn't mean to kick you between the thoughts.

Many believe that humans descended from apes. Fortunately, for the primates, there is no relation. As eternal spiritual beings, we progress from one life form to another: mineral, plant, insect, bird, mammal, and human. Life after life, our awareness expands until we discover our true nature as soul, which leads us to divine love.

Humans can be quite ridiculous. We look at birds and want to fly, so we build an airplane. "Wow," everyone says, "that's awesome. What an accomplishment. Now we can fly." We forget that birds have been flying for millions of years, don't burn fossil fuels, and generously fertilize our environment as they soar the friendly skies. Splat! Whoops! Sorry, Mr. Mind.

The more time you spend looking at the clock, the further you are from your heart, love's true home, beyond time, space, and all things known.

Everything is exactly as it should be, or life wouldn't be the way that it is. Illusion prevails in our physical world, which has been designed to temper us. The outer world never changes; it fluctuates, constantly reorganizing matter. We, however, can change; and once we do, the world appears differently. Every answer lies within our hearts, love's true home.

Analysis, dissection, reasoning, calculation, comparison, deduction, probing, experimentation, theorizing, or postulating cannot reveal the intrinsic nature of things. The incessant mechanical mind strives to keep soul's attention fixated on things of the outer world lest it discover something beyond its temporal physical body: divine love residing in each and every heart.

Science marvels at light because it moves so fast when in fact, it is nothing more than a slowpoke. Your divine imagination is capable of transporting you instantly to an exotic planet billions of light years away.

Why study a light bulb when the sun shines overhead?

Within the deepest chamber of every heart, far beyond any measure, glows an inextinguishable flame of divine love.

We are not alone. In the same way that explorers in the Old World set out across the ocean to discover and explore the New World, the same activity has been occurring for eons on a galactic scale. There are visitors from other planets. Only the puny and cowardly ego of man considers itself to be the apex of all creation.

The only difference between an atom and a solar system is size. To truly understand this, a deeper, broader perspective is required. Catapult yourself high above the confines of the mind, pull your viewpoint way back, further than you've ever been, and you will see that love is everywhere.

Science studies objects that are in motion, thereby only measuring the aftereffects known as events. This is the same as analyzing a pile of doggy-doo long after the pup has moved on to greener pastures. A little too late with a not-so-favorable lingering aroma describes science very well, yet it claims to know so much.

Words such as size, distance, before, and after are meaningless to the heart. The mind attempts to attach some kind of "real" value to worldly things, which all pass away. The heart is eternal and free, a fountain of eternal love, not bound by measurement of any kind. If you wish to experience this freedom and joy, simply go "out of your mind," and dive into your heart.

A man discovers an acorn, for the very first time, resting on the ground. He becomes fixated on knowing its origin and its meaning. Off to a lab he goes where he peels, dissects, measures, weighs, hypothesizes, extrapolates, and expounds grand theories on its true nature. If only he had gazed toward the heavens upon discovering it and observed the oak tree.

Not long ago, we were told that the universe rotated around our planet and if we sailed too far into the ocean, we would fall off the edge. Now we know better. Every time we recognize one of mind's lies, it fabricates another tray of delightfully deceptive delicacies and serves it up as truth. Experience is the only teacher.

In the vast expanse of so-called space or nothingness lie innumerable cosmic worlds where every conceivable dream awaits us. Our divine imagination is capable of giving life to these invisible gifts from spirit.

Science is hilarious! The human eye can only see one-tenth of 1 percent of the electromagnetic spectrum, which means that most of life's activities go unseen; yet using very limited scientific tools, we interpret the visible parts and claim to know so much about life.

The intellect has amazing influences in our world. Science probes deep into the heart of matter, thinking the key to life's origins will be found there. I can't help but laugh. Whoops! I turned the sun off by mistake. How are things looking now? Since you can no longer see anything, I guess it doesn't "matter."

Only two things can travel faster than the speed of light. The first is our vivid imagination: it can transport us instantly to an exotic planet a billion light years away. The second is a carload of shoppers heading for the Boxing Day specials at Wal-Mart.

The concepts "nothing" and "space' are very interesting. To most people, they imply the absence of anything whatsoever: emptiness, a void. Within this empty space, however, lie innumerable worlds of wonder teeming with life and filled with divine love. I know this to be true because I visit these glorious places daily, and I see them glistening in the eyes of everyone I meet.

The so-called big bang theory is another one of mind's goofy ideas meant to keep humans looking outside of themselves for answers.

Science claims that gravity is a physical force that keeps our feet planted on the ground. My experience is that mind is a much greater force, which keeps our consciousness trapped in the lower worlds of time and space.

A rainbow is truly something wonderful to behold. The source of a rainbow lies far beyond the mind's eye, and its magnificence can only be experienced within your loving heart.

We create nothing original. Creation is merely an endless reassembling of prefabricated molecules. Nature is in a state of flux, constantly reorganizing matter to maintain balance. Things only differ in the worlds of duality, creating a sense of separation. There is no opposite of divine love, which permeates all life. To experience it fully, one must rise above the worlds of differences, literally out of the body and far beyond the mind.

If something is explained in complex terms, it is usually very distant from truth. Life is simple; love is all there is. Long, drawn-out explanations are but puny morsels offered by the mind to divert our attention to countless outer forms that all fade away like fog melting in the sun. Gaze into your heart, and behold the splendor of God's infinite love.

The expressions "time is of the essence" and "a waste of time" are examples of how ridiculous the mind can be. Some claim there is an unlimited amount of time; others say time is only relative, and some sages say that time doesn't even exist. It is more accurate to state that the mind is a waste of time.

Anything is possible. Truth lies within. Nothing has been hidden. Imagine the very best in your life, and take the necessary steps to make it a reality.

Science is a constant source of entertainment. Today, many are playing with genetics and the building blocks of life, looking for answers. I prefer to keep company with the master architect of these blocks.

Science is like a child who never grows up, always fascinated with the trinkets and baubles of the mind, and blind to the loving heart, love's true home, wherein lies true spiritual freedom.

How are you getting from point A to point B? You can get there as soon as you can in the most efficient manner, or you can enjoy all the adventures along the way with your spiritual senses fully awakened.

The mind loves to hypnotize humans with symbols; powerful images firmly implanted in religion, philosophy, metaphysics, science, art, literature, music, etc. Many are unaware that a symbol is merely a representative of something greater. It stands between you, the seeker, and the thing that it represents. Why stare at a painting while love's light shimmers in the waters of your golden heart?

In the lower worlds of duality, everything has its opposite. For this reason, it is human nature to compare everything: bigger, smaller, closer, farther, better, best, etc. You get the picture. By going beyond the mind, you can experience something that has no opposite and is incomparable: divine love, residing in your heart, right here, right now.

I love dichotomy. On the one hand, we know scientifically that opposites attract. Curiously, we also know from personal experience that like attracts like.

If humans hadn't witnessed birds in flight, chances are we wouldn't have any flying machines today.

The greatest thing ever proved by Einstein is that nothing can be absolutely proven. This makes sense when you consider the fact that love, residing far beyond the scope of the mechanical mind, is all there is.

There is an underlying theme behind most scientific quests. The very word underlying says so much about how most of science has completely missed the mark. Do you really think that by digging deeper and looking farther, you will find the answer to the source of life?

Science totally misunderstands light. The only difference between a firefly and a sun is size. Our sun doesn't generate light; it is a conduit for light. Science behaves like small child, regarding the sun as if it was a wall socket, believing it to be the source of electricity.

Chapter 8

The Power of Words

Words can build or destroy. Compliment someone, and they are uplifted; this is love in action. Ridicule another, and words become potent weapons. Words are real, have substance, can be measured, felt, and conjure up images steeped with emotion. When we look for the best in life and express ourselves in a loving fashion, our words can work wonders.

One of mind's many positive characteristics is human language, which can serve as a valuable communication tool. It does have its limitations: no one has ever been able to talk their way into heaven.

I love kids. Recently I was introduced to a young girl. I asked her how old she was. When she replied, "I am six years old," I responded with "Wow! You must be living a wonderful life because when I was your age, I was only four." Her parents broke into uproarious laughter, and she beamed with a remarkable brightness. Words imbued with kindness and love can work wonders.

The symptom of a very serious "staff" infection is when everyone in the office is bickering, bitching, and gossiping. Love cures all.

The words "sacred" and "scared" are formed from the same letters. The difference in meaning, however, is astonishing. You have the power to transform the talons of fear within your mind into a flame of everlasting love glowing in your heart. No one else can do it. It's all up to you. Oh, my! Look at how bright thou art, sweet soul.

Several of my friends have said that I have a way with words. It's the other way around. Words have their way with me.

Although it is true that love has no real words, a kind heart and gentle mind can imbue words with a vitality, nobility, and spark, which awaken the love within others and us.

Some people arise in the morning, pray to their God, ask for protection, and then pick up their weapons to wage war against their brothers and sisters. We are all heaven's children, and God doesn't play favorites. Consider putting your vile weapons away and shooting arrows of love from your heart instead.

It truly is a paradox to say one thing and do another, to extend kindness to a friend and think badly of another.

The use of the word "should" in our expression is actually a judgment in which we expect others to behave like us.

A young boy I know was telling me about his invisible friends. I smiled as he related his adventures with these remarkable beings. He asked me if I truly believed in their existence. "Of course," I replied. "It is obvious that your invisible friends are real because I can't see them."

I love the expression "You have nothing to lose." Sometimes, in its moment of weakness, the mind says something that makes sense.

There is no such thing as a capacity for love. Love can't be contained. Love has an unlimited capacity for you, sweet child of God.

Never judge a cover by its book.

The words I speak are spirit's breath infused with the essence of myself.

> Dear Mr. Opinion and Ms. Bad Advice:
> You're not a brush in my hair; you're more like head lice.
> Your lips keep on flappin' as your nasty spit flies,
> Go gaze in a mirror and eat your own lies.

"It's too good to be true" is actually a negative expression. If something is truly good, there should be no doubt whatsoever.

If ignorance is bliss, does it mean that bliss is ignorant? Who the heck came up with this ridiculous configurent?

Chapter 9

Out of My Mind

We all know that the mind can get unruly with anger, fear, doubt, impatience, jealousy, and greed. Toss a cup of lively emotion into the mix, and watch out! Whenever it goes off on a tangent, I squirt a shot of sparkling love lube into that feisty little machine, and all the negative stuff fades away.

The mind is very adept at using the news media to propagate its endless messages of worry, fear, suspicion, doubt, and tragedy, which keep us preoccupied with events in the outer world. This greatly pleases the mind because we forget to look within our hearts, where mind has no power and love reigns supreme.

Are you using your mind to study the mind? Have you considered that it might be a little biased, perhaps playing favorites? How about getting to the heart of the matter?

Whoops! I apologize, Mr. Mind. I didn't mean to kick you between the thoughts.

I hope you don't mind, Mr. Mind, but mind your own business. You know the old saying "What's mine is mind, and what's yours is mind"? That's way too much mind for me. Bonk! Whoops! Sorry, I just gave you a good clout with my humongous loving heart. I hope you don't mind.

If something appears to be unreasonable, you are most likely heading toward your heart, love's true home.

The mind has a desperate need to question while overlooking spirit's treasure: in each heart, love without measure.

The expression "There's a reason for everything" is another trick of mind intended to divert your attention away from the truth. Divine love has no reason, needs no reason, and is far beyond reason.

There is only one thing standing between you and divine love: the mechanical mind.

Beyond reason is one of my favorite places to visit. Every time I lose my mind, I find myself dwelling far beyond fleeting temporal thoughts, in the magical worlds of light and sound within my heart, love's true home.

A circle is an interesting construct of the mind. Making a conscious choice to enter or exit a circle is much different than unwittingly living inside someone else's circle.

The ego is wrapped up with itself in constant adulation: a frantic, self-indulgent, repugnant mindsturbation.

Mind can be our greatest ally or our worst enemy. When you express yourself, are you reflecting love and wisdom garnered from your personal experiences, or are you spewing forth lies and illusions, which have been injected into your consciousness by others through countless lifetimes?

I love smashing the unruly mind to bits. A machine can always be rebuilt.

Did I forget to remember, or did I remember to forget? We have to be on our toes, or the clever mind sees to it that we forget our true nature as soul, ensuring that we only remember things that are worth forgetting.

Allowing the mind to be our master is like eating Jell-O with chopsticks. Sure, we might get the occasional hint of flavor but end up hungry and unfulfilled with a huge mess waiting to be cleaned up.

> Hey mind!
> I know you love to calculate, postulate, and extrapolate,
> Measure this, measure that, king of chaos, you're such a brat.
> You deserve a real good whack, and with my heart, I'll do it:

I'll pour my love all over you and laugh as you
pass through it.

The uncontrolled mind spews out an endless stream of
sweetened bile, lots of yuck lathered with yum. Thought after
thought and mile after mile, I love to watch the space between
my thoughts, where spirit waits with a loving smile.

Today, I see a proliferation of systems focused on stilling the
mind, probing the mind, developing the mind, harnessing
the mind, dissecting the mind, and glorifying the mind. Jeez!
It's only a machine. Get beyond it! In the heart of every being
shines a golden sun: this is all we need to know. Mind attempts
to conceal truth by complicating the simplest of things.

An uncontrolled mind can be compared to an amusement
park. Wow! Look at all the fun rides and awesome games.
Meanwhile, behind the scenes, the ego dreams up elaborate
schemes to get dollars out of your wallet. Boot! Goodbye,
mind. Go mind your own business.

The mind is difficult for many to understand, yet it is nothing
more than a machine. As soul, we use it in tandem with our
physical body and astral body (emotions) as an instrument
of perception and expression while gaining experience in
the lower worlds. Eventually, soul discards these devices
and perceives directly rather than viewing things as being
separate and outside of itself.

The mind literally fears nothing. It is terrified to death of
nothing because within nothing lies everything.

A few like to lead, but most like to follow.
Many seek things that are empty and hollow.
The circle expands as the lies keep on growing.
One hell of a party, the clever mind's throwing.

What's the difference between a man with a hammer, a man with a chain saw, a man with a computer, and a man with a mind? Essentially, they are the same. In each instance, he has a tool with limited capabilities. The last one, the man with the mind, sometimes thinks he is the tool.

A highly developed intellect has nothing to do with true intelligence. Let's not confuse the workings of the mechanical mind with consciousness. Intelligence blends a loving, compassionate heart with noble thoughts, kind acts, and a trained mind. Society worships the mind, which can be a great tool but is a ruthless master. Sometimes losing my mind is a liberating experience!

Allowing mind to be our master is like being locked in an outhouse. Sure, after a while, you get used to the cramped space, the stench, and darkness; but there are better places to be. Gather your fears, and flush them down the toilet bowl of oblivion. Wipe away the ghostly apparitions from your mind, and behold divine love residing in your golden heart.

"Look at me!" squawks the ego, wobbling like a duck drunk on whisky, feathers flying every which way, leaving in its wake a slimy trail and a lingering odor. It moves ever forward, plotting the next catastrophe, all the while thinking it knows everything. The only escape is to go out of my mind.

> I live only once, so why does it matter?
> I take what I can, and I load up my platter.
> I am the boisterous mind and love getting fatter.
> I always avoid the heart of the matter.

The mechanical mind out of control has a singular goal: to show you the pieces and make hidden the whole.

The mind is incapable of being satisfied. One momentary gratification always leads to another craving. The radiant heart, however, is always at peace with love—satisfaction guaranteed!

Mind over matter? They are one and the same: a play on words yet another mind game.

Moments that define us? I am soul, child of God, and full of love: beyond definition, boundless, and free.

The mind is inextricably immersed in the chaotic worlds of matter, time, and space. It always works toward future events and must have goals and aspirations. Soul, which lives in the eternal now, has no goals. It has its being in divine love, so it strives for nothing.

Hey, you! Whatever it is that you are thinking, you are not that. Stop thinking right now! Can you do it? Whatever it is that you are not thinking is your true self.

> It's a phony kind of egg-stacy, living deep within
> your shell.
> I don't know why you do it mind, turning heaven
> into hell.
> You're tricky, and I don't trust you;
> I'm a love cop, and I'll bust you.

Anything imaginable already exists. Thought is a reflective process whereby we "shine our light" onto prefabricated states of consciousness and awaken them from their slumber. Ideas are elements of the universal mind, a vast repository of latent images that become flavored and emotionally charged with our unique qualities whenever we "think."

What do you think it would be like to stop thinking? I'm not talking about stilling the mind or controlling your thoughts; you are still in the mind with that approach. I'm talking about no thoughts whatsoever, far beyond its ghostly walls. Think about it! How about getting to the heart of the matter?

An empty mind is a great vessel to pour a whole lotta love into. Dump out the crap, and pump in the joy. Bring it on!

The mechanical mind can be likened to training wheels on a bicycle. Unlike children who rise above their fears and learn to ride free as the wind without them, many humans cling tenaciously to the mind as they wobble precariously from life to life wondering why they are not free.

The purpose of the mind or the mind's ego trip? Who steers at the helm of your mystic ship?

A thing is only big when compared to something smaller. It is insignificant when compared to something much larger. The mind thinks it knows everything, but there is nothing to know! Love is all there is.

There are many who are attached to the mind and always want to defend it.

"It's now or never." One more meaningless statement slithers out of the pathetic mechanical mind. It is always now; there is no such thing as "never."

Oh, oh! My insurmountable madness is skirting much too close to the edge of sanity. I prefer to lose my mind and take a long swim in the warm, soothing waters of your loving heart.

The mind hates to be alone and always seeks attention.

Whenever I boot my mind in the tush, I feel a mighty loving rush.

It is impossible to pour love into a mind that is filled to the brim with murky illusions. What happens if I toss my humongous loving heart into it? Splash! Ahhh, that feels much better.

The mind would have you think that "mind candy" is something awesome, something real. When the body dies, it takes the mind and candy with it. I prefer to drink from the heavenly nectar of love flowing eternally out of the heart of God.

Some say that love is blind. From my perspective, mind is blind and love sees all.

Another one of mind's comical expressions is "Two heads are better than one." Yikes! My experience has been that two heads often lead to twice as many mistakes.

The mechanical mind is very crafty. It considers itself to be the ultimate thing. It wants us to focus on things of the outer world, on other people and events outside of ourselves. The mind is exuberant when we are worried, fearsome, greedy, and anxious: anything to prevent us from exploring our true nature.

Have you ever heard of the mind's eye and how awesome it is? I don't trust that creepy Cyclops because it has its eye on one thing only: itself, the big ego. I choose to see with my spiritual eye, which is always on the lookout for love and for you!

The mind's never-ending quest is to know. Unfortunately, all knowledge is a few dollars short of wisdom, which lies in your heart, love's true home.

Often, the mind will come up with ridiculous sayings such as "It's like trying to find a needle in a haystack." With my imagination, I can easily see a haystack in a needle.

When I view life via the filter of thoughts and images provided to me by the universal mind, I see all kinds of problems. When I go out of my mind and dive into my heart, all I see is love.

An unruly mind has been likened to a monkey in a cage. Comparing mind to a monkey in a cage is too high a compliment; it's nothing more than a cage. A monkey has more freedom.

A crazy expression touted by the self-centered mind is "Imitation is the sincerest form of flattery." When one strives to become a caricature of somebody else, frustration and disappointment are sure to follow. Behold the splendor of your true self. Settle for nothing less.

"Cleanliness is next to Godliness." What next? Another meaningless statement slithers from that myopic monarch, the mechanical mind. Soul can surely bask in the glory of God's love light, but nothing whatsoever could possibly sit next to God.

The mind is like a box of Lego. We can create worlds of wonder for ourselves or allow others to build walls around us.

Are you a legend in your own mind? Do you consider your mind to be legendary? Dare to lose your mind, and in your heart, you'll find something quite extraordinary.

A mind under control can be an incredible tool. You can do crazy things with it if you have a loving heart.

I've had it with this pathetic cerebral cortex. I'm diving heart first into your spinning love vortex.

"It's do or die!" Here we go again, a goofy saying by the mind. I am soul, eternal, boundless, and free; so dying is out of the question. Secondly, I would rather be than do; therefore I am. Go play with somebody your own size, pesky little mind: good luck finding something that small.

Why clamor and scramble for dry, tasteless crumbs offered up by the mechanical mind, while a heavenly loaf of love leavens in the holy chamber of your golden heart?

A finely honed mind is like the vaulter's pole: it can take you to the top, but you have to let it drop before passing through heaven's gate.

The expression "quit while you're ahead" terrifies me. The head is the problem to begin with, and to quit now would mean a longer incarceration in Gloomsville. I'm hopping on the magic carpet of love in your heart and zooming off into spirit's wondrous skies.

> Cultured and polished, so suave and debonair,
> You stand amidst a cyclone, moving not a hair.
> You're quite the handsome fellow, your lips a wicked leer,
> You strike me with your dagger eyes and inject me with your fear.
> I've finally moved beyond you, mind, to a heaven high above, far from this room that you call home, a prison without love.

The myopic mind is only capable of viewing its contents and incapable of seeing what contains it.

The heart shines like a golden sun; the mind is incognito. One path leads to precious love, and the other strokes the ego.

Today, someone told me that I must be out of my mind to act in the ways that I do. I thanked her for the loving compliment.

Positive thinking has its place in the world of the mind, the world of fleeting ideas. In the world of my heart, love's true home, thought has no place whatsoever.

Do you mind if I coagulate your thought? No matter what you think it's not.

Mind is incapable of comprehending the concept of "nothing" because it imagines itself to be a big, wonderful, and irreplaceable "something."

Recently I got tired of being a puppet on a string. I'm not sure why, but I woke up and then it all made sense: until that point, I'd spent my life deep in mind's pretense. I found my heart. I dove straight in, and much to my surprise, I landed smack dab in the center of spirit's loving eyes.

The ego is a master at expressing itself through personalities. It loves to say, "Look at me!" Our world teems with false heroes in which some sport figures, politicians, and celebrities are worshiped because of so-called "great" accomplishments. A true hero acts from a loving heart, without regard for self, and sacrifices all for another. Heroism seeks not attention or praise; it is divine love in action.

Many worship and praise the mind and consider it to be sublime. From my perspective, it's more of a crime and closer to being sublemon.

Mind is only a machine, but somehow, it has become the ultimate weapon of mass seduction.

I love giving my mind a swift hard kick right between the thoughts.

Is thought something unique and original that arises from deep within us? Or is thought a reflective process whereby we experience in a personal manner something that already exists?

There is no difference between up and down: stand on your head, and it's all turned around. So get down, get up, and start all over again: it never makes sense when you think with your brain.

Everything has its place. I'm still trying to find one for my mind, but all that I have found to date has been much too large to accommodate.

Every time you praise the mind, you are worshiping a machine.

Chapter 10

Smiledorphins

Whenever someone smiles at you in a sincere loving manner, accept it graciously, and share it with another. Unleash your smiledorphins! Release the liberating power, wisdom, and love residing in the holy chamber of your golden heart.

Your smile is a golden sun radiating sparks of effervescent love: a gift from spirit, which invigorates and sustains all life. Shine forth, sweet one.

I am forever infected by the power and wisdom radiating from your immaculate, contagious smiles. My grateful heart soaks in every atom of your sweet love.

Your mysterious face is a wonderful, never-ending story. Each smile and every twinkle in your eyes are a new chapter forever melting my heart.

Smiles are connected to the eyes, mirrors of the soul. When we smile, our eyes sparkle with an effervescence and warmth, which endears us to and uplifts those around us.

Whenever someone makes us smile, pleases us, or inspires us, we are enjoying a reflection of ourselves: full of love, beauty, goodness, and grace. Welcome to the inimitable splendor of your true self, O precious soul.

A genuine smile is like a warm rain shower followed by a glorious rainbow. It cleanses, invigorates, and enriches the lives of everyone it touches.

At home or office, at work or play, share your smile with someone today.

Whenever your incandescent smile gently whispers its fragrant breath, the flame within my heart bursts into a raging fire; and suddenly, I am flying on the magic carpet of your love.

How high can I fly?
Beyond every known sky, where I soak up the
warmth of your generous smile and hover in the
light of your radiant eyes.
Then I'm off like a comet soaring much higher,
I abandon my wings and dive into your fire.

Whenever we experience fortune or grace in our lives, the
light and sound of God is smiling upon us.

I love basking in the radiance of your neon smile as it
illuminates my grateful heart.

I woke up this morning with a smile upon my face; I perceived
the beauty and felt the warm grace of your love.

Take your frown, and flip it upside down; now you have a
smile that you can share for a while.

Chapter 11

Mad Planet

Someone asked me where I was from. I told them I was born in a spectacular place called Synchroni City and somehow ended up in Tena City. I plan on returning to my birthplace soon.

Planet Earth is a simmering pot of spicy soup, and we are the ingredients. Dip in your ladle, and drink heartily from this potpourri of dazzling flavors. What does it taste like to you?

Life could be likened to a cow. It always seems greener on the udder side, and there's an endless stream of bull to contend with.

Perhaps our wings fell off from lack of use. For some reason, flying has taken a backseat to crawling, crying, whining, complaining, backbiting, groveling, and sniveling.

I'm trying to figure out a way to make this nanosecond last longer. Whoosh! Oh, well. Here comes another one.

Although my name is Sri Gawn Tu Fahr, I have discovered that I haven't gone nearly far enough. It's a long way to nowhere, and the last time I arrived, I didn't realize I was there until long after I had departed.

Many die for what others believe in. We have been programmed to follow goals created for us by religion, culture, government, family, and peers. For the few who pursue their own goals, life and death are inseparable.

Today, there are many who are willing to die for their country, their religion, and their beliefs. I wonder how many are willing to live for what they believe in?

Spirit's loving embrace transforms the noxious weeds of tyranny into a meadow of fragrant wild flowers.

Be careful not to get too far ahead of yourself, or you may end up spending the rest of your life trying to catch up.

Are you feeling befuddled or slightly
bemuddled?
Does it feel like you're standing in a dark gooey
puddle?
Leap out of that hole and fling off your boots!
Climb up that tree and gobble down fruits.
I see you there smiling, perched way up high,
free as a bird, bright sun in the sky.

We are all aware of it, but few talk about it, and many are actively engaged in it. It is everywhere: greed! This negative passion of the mind rules many humans who believe that they must possess things and control others to feel fulfilled. The spiritual antidote for greed is divine love residing in your golden heart.

You've got quite a life; I like the way you live it. I like the way you laugh, and I like the way you give it.

I can't remember much of what he was talking about. I think it was advice on how to be a good listener.

Patriotism can be a two-edged sword. On one hand, it creates a sense of unity, strength, and idealism. On the other hand, it pits brother against brother, sister against sister, and nation against nation.

A fact, for sure, is nothing true. It's just a single point of view.

Meaningful change in the outer world won't occur from efforts of individuals or groups trying to force others to do it their way, no matter how noble their intentions might be. Spiritual change occurs within each individual and is reflected outwardly. As more beacons light up, the brighter life becomes.

Did you know that in India alone, there are thousands of gods and goddesses, yet there is only one true God?

The bulk of humanity marches like ants serving the needs of their precious queen bee, more commonly referred to as the mind.

Some are predicting major disasters, upheaval, and death in 2012. Surely you jest! There is no death for soul. You flounder within this imagined darkness and try to draw others into your fear. Behold your true spiritual nature, and bask in the brilliance of love's flame glowing forever in your heart.

Many human beings are driven to possess physical objects. Why do we want these things? Do we require them for our spiritual growth? We have been programmed for eons by religion, education, government, parents, and our peers to acquire material goods? Mind rules on planet Earth, seeking only self-gratification. We live primarily in a "me" world.

Is your aura a toxic emission, a vile imposition, or a soothing, uplifting, divine love transmission?

What is it about my life you would like me to change so you can feel better about your life? Sorry, it doesn't work that way.

When we rely on others to make us feel good, we are in for a rocky ride. We don't need the approval of others to enjoy life. Divine love resides in the center of our glorious hearts, and vanquishes all fears. Take a look right now, and drink deeply, resplendent soul.

I scratch my head in wonderment whenever an adult asks a child, "What are you going to be when you grow up?" The pesky mind wants us to look to the future and forget the now.

Where some only see a rosebud, I behold a spiritual flower, soul in full resplendent bloom.

Many great historical figures thought out of the box and presented original ideas that challenged contemporary thought and inspired the world. Soon thereafter, many of these earth-shaking concepts were repackaged and sold back to the world by unscrupulous wallet hounds in the name of profit.

If things, people, and events in the world inspire you, know this: the source of this inspiration rests in your golden heart. Everything you experience in the outer world is a reflection of your inner states of consciousness.

The problem with this circle I'm in is that I always come back to the same place over and over again. Jeez, I wish I could understand what reincarnation is "wheely" all about.

It is interesting how some doctors can have lots of patients yet be very short on patience when interacting with them.

I am sure there are many good reasons for reason, but for some reason, I can't come up with any right now. Am I being unreasonable?

René Descartes, seventeenth century physicist, physiologist, mathematician, and philosopher, was famous for saying, "I think, therefore I am." No one can think unless they already exist. How about "I am, therefore I think?"

One sure way to deepen your rut is to give in to lust and top up your glut.

Looking for great investment advice? Inject a healthy dose of "adventure" capital into yourself. Toss those coins of love into the treasure chest within your heart, and rejoice as your precious nest egg grows.

Once you discover your true spiritual nature, you'll stop worrying about where you're going and when you're going to get there because you will have finally arrived. Welcome to where you've always been.

A loving heart leaves a beautiful mark without intending any gain, while the mechanical mind has selfish goals and always leaves a stain.

There isn't much point in kissing a mirror; a reflection is nothing like the original.

God was not created in our image. Whenever someone addresses God as "Him" or "Lord," they are referring to one of the lower deities. The Supreme Being is neither male nor female; God does not dwell in the world of duality.

I can't wait to find out how old I'm going to be when I grow up.

If it wasn't for our differences, we would be identical.

Are you kiddin'? Every secret is a lie because truth cannot be hidden.

> There once was a mind from mud hollow, which
> had depths that were much less than shallow.
> It slithered and spewed awful things oh-so-crude
> and forever continues to wallow.

The natural consequence of "freaking in" is "freaking out."

> An angry mind is a dark syringe,
> It poisons the heart and makes soul cringe.
> It injects us with fear and fills us with doubt,
> Preventing sweet love from cascading out.

If you truly want to make sense of what's going on "out there," simply take a look at what's going on in your heart.

Are you half asleep or half awake? They are not one and the same.

Instead of trying to overcome something, why not undercome it, thereby saving lots of valuable time (which doesn't exist anyway)?

> Details are for microscopes, distances for telescopes, murky depths for periscopes, and promises for broken hopes.
> They're all mind's lies for human dopes, so throw away that useless rope.
> Open up your heart to God, and let spirit's river flow.
> Love is what you are, sweet soul; this is all you need to know.

Chapter 12

Fast-Food Salvation

No one can save us. Many await the return of a great redeemer, savior, or messiah. This idea originates in the mind, falsely promising that someone else will solve the world's problems. The mind presents this powerful idea to divert your attention away from your true self, causing you to look to the future and hope for salvation. There is nothing to save. As a child of God, you are already free.

Some motivational speakers are well-paid entertainers. Their motivation is to get $$$ from the pockets of others through the use of grandiose intellectual pronouncements, sparkling smiles, twinkling eyes, and animated gestures. Relying on external sources for answers is the first step in our spiritual growth. Eventually, we discover that truth and love reside within our hearts, love's true home.

If a teacher, counselor, guru, instructor, leader of any profession or spiritual teaching acts as if he or she knows it all, chances are they know very little. Boot! Next!

Spirituality cannot be bought or taught; it can only be caught. Divine love is splashing around in your glorious heart right now; so pull out your magic fishing rod, start trolling for joy, and share your bountiful catch with others.

Some claim that they can teach you (for a price) how to "increase your capacity to attract and keep real love." This is preposterous. Love cannot be kept or contained. It is not a something outside of ourselves, which we attract. Love resides in every heart, can't be bought or sold at any price, and has an unlimited capacity for you sweet soul.

I have learned that one does not have to be a saint, guru, or master to recognize, enjoy, and share the beauty, wonder, and glory of God's divine love.

All religions serve a purpose and vary in their teachings. They are all paths, but alas, they are constructs of the mind, destined to perish. Love, the source of all life, resides in every heart, far beyond religion, philosophy, metaphysics, science, and the mind itself.

Many "wallet hounds" offer spiritual salvation, financial salvation, and emotional salvation. Salvation comes packaged in various sizes, shapes, colors, aromas, etc. Fortunately, there is nothing to save. As soul, you are already free. Toss that wallet where it really counts—into the glorious waters of your loving heart.

Today, guru-mania runs rampant. Our worldly landscape teems with experts, specialists, gurus, teachers, guides, leaders, and saviors, many of them claiming to have the answers to life's problems. This is the mind doing its best work. Authentic masters all say the same thing: the source of life and the solution to every problem lives in every heart, love's true home.

Which teachings do you follow? The wisdom of the prophets or the wise guys bent on profit?

Much is being said about harnessing the power of attraction. Love can't be saddled or reigned in. There is nothing to attract. Relax, gaze inward, and behold your true nature. Love begets only love when your heart is open.

I am Sri Ego. I know it all! I am the door to truth so don't interrupt! Listen to me and do as I say! Buy my book and dvd. Follow my 96 rules to enlightenment. Where is my lunch? I've been perched on this pedestal for hours and my butt is killing me. Don't ask such stupid questions. Will you ever learn? Repeat after me, "Sri Ego, Sri Ego, only through you can we go."

Some teachers are agents of the mind, offering intellectual crumbs to the spiritually famished. Words only get you thinking. No teaching is worth a pinch of mouse poop unless it is imbued with divine love. Rise above mental ideas, and discover who you truly are by expressing yourself fully from the heart. Love is all there is.

It has been stated that when some saints reach an exalted state and are poised for true mastership, they fall prey to vanity, a most insidious negative passion of the mind. Allowing oneself to be worshipped, admired, and put on a pedestal creates an illusion that one is better than others, guaranteeing a swift, hard fall. Humility is the sweetest of holy qualities.

Some people seek out psychics hoping to discover who they were in a past life. Knowing who you are in the ever present moment of the now is much more revealing and provides greater benefits. Only you can discover who you are and what your true purpose in life is.

Today, I observe a number of crafty charlatans promising fast-food solutions to the spiritually hungry. Truth can't be sold or told. Fancy words and grandiose gestures merely stimulate the intellect and get you thinking. Only by surfing the cosmic waves in the ocean of your loving heart are you able to transcend life's problems and discover your true spiritual nature.

An authentic master is patient and compassionate. Impatience is one of the many faces of anger, which is not conducive to healthy relationships. A good teacher inspires through example, not just flowery words, sparkling eyes, and animated gestures.

Why study an aura? Look within at the source of your aura. Behold God's love living in your heart, and allow spirit to be your guide. An aura is but one manifestation of your true self. Why gaze at a candle when the sun shines above? Your golden heart illuminates all darkness and vanquishes all questions.

Today, I see many self-appointed representatives of God. Love is God's sole representative and glows forever in your golden heart.

Since love is all there is, there are no such thing as secrets.

Messages are a dime a dozen. Some so-called spiritual messengers in today's world are looking to make a whole lot more than a dime. Why pay for something you already have?

The secret to financial success, the secret to spiritual freedom, the secret to happiness, the secrets of manifesting, the secret to this, and the secret to that. Many are willing to sell these secrets for profit. I am wary of those who tell or sell so-called secrets, especially in light of the fact that truth cannot be hidden.

Much is being said about "attracting and keeping real love" as if it was something outside of us. Love cannot be kept or influenced. Love is all there is, sweet soul. You are love.

Self-proclaimed gurus are everywhere, promising to have answers to our problems. Life is simple; we exist because of God's love. Look at your brothers and sisters and rejoice. We are all children of God.

Love is the answer to every question, challenge, and problem. The mind always complicates the simplest things.

A good teacher inspires and strives to bring out the best in a student. If your teacher is arrogant, belittling, or sarcastic and allows him or herself to be hoisted onto a pedestal and worshipped, consider shopping around. An authentic teacher is a guide who encourages us to bring out what we already have: sweet, sweet love!

Chapter 13

Gratitude and Sharing

It's amazing what we can do with love and astonishing what love can do with us.

Very few are aware that a true gift has two components. A gift given in love must also be received in love in order for a spiritual transaction to be successful.

The giving of love is a spiritual expression of the greatest significance.

The sharing of food with others is a sublime expression of divine love.

Allowing another person to express their point of view is a vital step in our personal spiritual development.

Sharing is the loving child of gratitude's sweet breath. When we behold spirit's lustrous splendor living in the heart of every blessed moment, we naturally want to share.

I am a mischievous, happy little love pump spreading spirit's love. There is no end in sight as I drench you with luscious droplets of sweet liquid joy.

Thou art an everlasting candle forever dripping love into my heart.

I love the way you compliment yourself when you tell me how wonderful I am.

A single drop of water from your sparkling loving ocean sways my heart forever with a gentle graceful motion.

Joy fills me as I sprinkle shimmering effervescent atoms of divine love into the exhilarating eyes of life.

The degree to which we experience love and personal freedom in our lives is directly proportional to how much love and freedom we grant others.

I have so much love to share that I carry two large buckets, one in each hand. I use them to catch the overflow spilling out of my heart, but it's not enough, as my love splashes every which way. I could use some help. Wanna lighten my load?

I am a love-filled overflowing cup. Even if you tip me over, I can never be emptied because spirit flows through my heart constantly.

You are the thunder in my wings and the lightning in my eyes; your love's the only fuel I need to fly these wondrous skies.

At the exact moment that I was born, I was blessed with the most incredible gift anyone could possibly receive: life.

I am flying so high in the depths of your precious heart. My love for thee has no measure. Thou art my treasure and only pleasure. How I cherish thee, sweet spirit.

Your exquisite beauty turns me on like a radio, my grateful heart broadcasting spirit's message of sweet love to all who will listen.

God graciously bestows everything I have to share upon me. Spirit fills me up with love until I overflow to others. As it splashes out of my heart, more pours in to replace what I have shared.

Did you know that whenever you compliment someone in a sincere fashion, you are stirring the love pudding in his or her heart?

Are you feeling receptive and generous today? Why not saturate yourself with swirling helixes of cosmic love atoms and share them with others through loving thoughts, feelings, and actions?

When we acknowledge another person in a positive way, we are channeling spirit's love, doing God's work, uplifting others, and making our world a better place.

Today, as the sun shines and the rain falls, I recognize spirit's bounty within each and every one of you.

In the midst of our planetary madness, one thing is for sure: life is simple and love lives in every heart.

It is a supreme joy and honor for me to reflect spirit's sweet love residing in your golden heart.

Accepting spirit's love is like receiving a box of the world's most exquisite chocolates. The box is bottomless, and the supply is endless. I am moved to share them with everyone. Want some?

Our thoughts, feelings, bodies, and possessions don't belong to us. Everything is bestowed by the grace of God. Generosity is sharing with others what spirit has given us.

Pets are wonderful teachers. Observe a dog on its walk through the park: so curious, soaking up every fresh scent with glee as if it's reading the latest headline in a newspaper. We would all benefit from being like dogs in this respect—marveling at the many wonders in life and immersing ourselves in the spiritual opportunities awaiting us at every turn.

When giving and sharing, if you do it in the name of spirit or God, amazing things happen.

Sometimes the love I feel for life is so overwhelming that tears of joy and gratitude stream out of my eyes, glide down my chest, and drip into my heart.

If you are enjoying the light, spark, and goodness that you are feeling from others at this moment, it's because you are seeing a reflection of yourself as soul, full of love, beauty, and grace. Give yourself a great big hug!

Today, I am a happy little honeybee, grinning and merrily buzzing along as I sprinkle liquid rainbows of sweet love nectar everywhere I go.

Behold your precious seeds of sweet love: such a wondrous gift! Plant them in the fertile garden of your divine imagination, and rejoice as your tears of gratitude enliven them. Watch them sprout with glee as they reach for the nourishing love light in your heart.

Sharing the same flame is such a fun game to play with you. Laughing, holding hands, and running along the shores of love as trumpets sing our names from the sparkling heavens high above.

The acts of giving and receiving have different dynamics than the acts of giving and taking.

Spirit has a way of giving us exactly what we need at exactly the right moment, whether we want it or not. Relax, be open, and know that all is fine.

Love is totally out of my control, and I thank God for that.

Once we stop taking, we start learning about giving and receiving.

Love is a gift from God, which we share with others. The supply is unlimited, so drink deeply and fill your cup until it overflows to those around you.

Every time I give and share, I remember why I love and care.

Infinite, delightful mysteries art thou, precious snowflake woman. I am mesmerized by your beauty and grace. I laugh and revel in your every facet.

I rely on nothing because I have everything. Love flows from my heart into yours and pours back into mine.

You are so tree-mendous babe; I'm really rooting for you. I can't leaf you alone, my love; your fruits, my heart's desire. I'm branching out in all directions and reaching for your fire.

When you live a life full of love, your heart radiates sparkling atoms of truth, which serve to uplift all mankind and set you free.

What does it mean to be a channel for spirit? When we open our hearts to spirit, love flows through us and we are sharing God's gifts. Can it get any better than this?

Your grateful heart is a shimmering waterfall of love, cascading into the hearts of others. Spirit shines through conscious souls to light the worlds.

Beauty truly lies within. When we see it within ourselves, our hearts become like suns, radiating love to everyone and everything we encounter on our journey back home.

Being able to accept a gift graciously is a wonderful gift in itself.

We can always tell when someone touches our hearts. Love energizes us and uplifts our entire being as well as those around us.

We radiate goodness and joy when we shine from within. Love is about giving and sharing. My heart is bursting with love and gratitude. Thank you, spirit, for this moment.

When our heart is open and our mind relaxed, spirit is able to flow through us more easily, uplifting and inspiring the loving souls we encounter on our journey called life.

Chapter 14

Freedom

I didn't realize who I was until I stopped being who I wasn't.

Are you tired of spending your life preoccupied with the outer world, mesmerized as you watch other people's videos displaying on the screen of your mind? Get up, go upstairs, and become a divine projector. Create your own Oscar-worthy film, and give yourself the starring role as the perfect lover.

Freedom can't be found, and love can't be attained. Both lie waiting in your heart, far beyond your brain.

I stumbled in complete darkness, lost and alone. Suddenly, out of nowhere, a spark of you appeared, a flickering firefly of love. As I gazed upon thee, a sun flew out of my heart. All darkness was dispelled, vanquished were my fears, and free flowing were my tears of joy.

We form a kaleidoscopic potpourri of shimmering love atoms intermingling in a joyous dance of divine ecstasy.

I am a profusion of whirling cosmic love atoms forever dancing in your heart.

If my love gets any higher, I'll have to pull out my divine excavator and start digging for heaven.

I am not on a mission. I am love's mission.

Our divine imagination is a magic carpet ride into our hearts. Summon your courage, fly away, and venture forth into love's glorious depths. Freedom has always been ours, but the mind would have us think otherwise. If we want love, we must give love, because love is all there is.

What you consider to be a hurdle is nothing more than a turtle in a girdle. Mind has a way of keeping us bound, making us blind to the light and sound, where deep in our hearts true love is found.

I'm a supersonic love tonic, a philosophical word comic raining down from the sky.

What a cute little birdie. I know you feel very comfortable in that warm, secure nest. The mind has been spoon-feeding you tender morsels of yummy lies for countless lives, and life is so sweet. Boot! Whoops! Sorry. I didn't mean to kick you out of your nest. Oh, my! You're flying! Hmmm, I bet you didn't know you had wings.

If you wanna love me, you gotta love you.

If you truly want to be free, simply allow others to be.

I surf the rainbows in your smile; forever, I am free as I dive deep into your heart, love's sweet ecstasy.

Many are blind to mind's confinement and attempt to fight the system from within. One must transcend all prison walls to experience true spiritual freedom.

Sometimes my mind is a swirling vortex of infinite insanities, and it sure feels good to bust loose from its incarceration and rise above it on occasion.

> Toss your fear, despair, and all things forlorn into the horn of your unicorn.
> There's one in your heart, and it's a magical beast. Start smacking your lips; it's time for a feast.

God provided us with feet so we can stand, walk, and choose our experiences in life. We realize this once we stop crouching, crawling, and cowering. Simply give that ole mind a hearty kick right between the thoughts. Ka-boom! Stand up and experience the glory of true spiritual freedom simmering in your loving heart.

Mind is to soul as human is to dog. We get to go for walks, get fed, and get petted; you know the story. Mind always has a leash in hand to pull us back lest we wander beyond its limitations and discover freedom in our love-filled hearts.

I will be much sweeter after tasting thee.

I love to lose my mind. A little freedom is a good thing once in a while.

I just performed a triple bypass surgery on my mind by pumping it up with love, power, and wisdom. That feels much better! A little bit of freedom is a good thing once in a while.

There is very little difference between the computer in front of you and your mind; both are machines. Who is operating these machines? As humans, we often find that mind, a ruthless master, is running the show. If you truly seek freedom, allow divine love in your heart to be your guide, and that pesky mind will bother you no more.

The most insidious prison is one in which the inmates think they are free. Yoo-hoo everybody! Wake up!

In today's world, there is a frenzied clamor for the acquisition of personal power, which lies in the domain of the insecure, cowardly, and pesky mind. When soul combines power with love and wisdom, freedom is realized and it becomes a balanced, effective, and dynamic vehicle for spirit's love. Now we're talking.

If you are referring to personal freedom, I keep mine. I have learned that if I allow others their freedom, my freedom grows. If you refer to spiritual freedom, it cannot be given or taken.

I don't rely on approval from others to feel good about myself, so most of the time I am in a loving space and hear spirit's gentle whispers.

Whenever we try to change someone, it means that we aren't accepting ourselves. Come on! You totally rawk! Learn to love yourself, and as you do, your heart will open like a flower smiling at the sun.

Unlike planet Earth, my spiritual environment is impervious to pollution. In my worlds of wonder, every ray of light and every celestial sound is completely imbued with the freshness of spirit's loving breath.

A spiritual creation of a high magnitude is made manifest when soul allows spirit's love to enter and flow through its heart.

Forgiveness opens the floodgates of love within our hearts. It is an important step in liberating ourselves from the shackles of the mechanical mind.

Much has been written about attachment and how to rise above it. This has nothing to do with our possessions. Being detached means not getting overly stressed by our failures or too excited by our successes. To be detached is to be balanced, free, and filled with love.

My faith is based on experience, not hope. When I am relaxed, my heart speaks and I feel spirit's love. When I listen to its gentle inner guidance, all is well in my life.

The word "democracy" has lost its original meaning. In today's world, it often means the freedom to get away with as much as you can without getting caught.

I don't believe in God; it is a delicious knowing based on personal experience.

I enjoy the childlike spirit within myself: good natured, healthy, curious, and active. I love to frolic, tease, laugh, and play with all of you.

Constantly changing my routine is part of my daily routine. Life never gets boring.

Spirit heals, not people. We are vehicles for spirit's love. A true healer is humble and grateful for the opportunity to act as a channel for spirit's loving energy.

Behold a golden sun within your heart. Let it shine forth, and know that you are a perfect soul. Allow spirit's love to set you free.

I am perched high atop the wonderful loving wings of spirit and grinning broadly as I zoom effortlessly across the heavens. Come on, everybody! Hop on board! Let's travel together on a glorious, fun-filled adventure and explore the magical worlds within our golden hearts.

When spirit, the holy sound and light of heaven, issues forth from the heart of God, it is pure and singular. As it crosses the threshold into the lower worlds of duality, it is split into three rays. Hence, we have Brahma, Vishnu, and Shiva (Hindu trinity); Father, Son, and Holy Ghost (Christian trinity); and many others. The true God is singular, indivisible, one.

I am much too busy being free to worry about my earthly existence.

I bow to no one. I bask joyfully in the glory of God's loving light and sound.

When one is truly "being," he or she is no longer of this world. The state of pure being is far beyond physical bodies, duality, and the worlds of fleeting thoughts.

You tread on nobody, you harm not a soul, and your aim is the highest for the good of the whole.

You are love. Nothing more need be said in the ever-present moment of the now.

Away to the far country I am bound, atop your wings of light and sound. Now I know where love is found.

When we judge someone, we are attempting to extinguish the spiritual essence of that being, and our personal freedom is diminished.

> There's nothing that I have to do and nothing
> that I have to see.
> Deep in your golden heart, my love, is the only
> place for me.

For me, love is not more or less than anything. It is the only thing; it is my everything.

These days, many things that are considered priceless are in fact worthless. Love is free.

I don't like being here now. It means I'm stuck right here, right now. I need a change of scene. I need more freedom. Henceforth, I'm going to be there now and be here later.

There are many different ways to pray. When I pray, I open my heart to spirit and allow its love to flow through me. Spirit decides what is best, and I do nothing whatsoever to color its wisdom with my personal wants, wishes, or desires.

Trying to still the mind is a waste of time; by its very nature, the mind is a mechanical chatterbox, so why try and bring it to a halt? Going out of my mind is the perfect solution for me. When I lose my mind, I soar high above it and am oblivious to its ghostly temptations. Dive into your glorious heart right now; enjoy the love and freedom that has always been yours.

Once I learned to accept spirit's love, I had no more questions.

Give yourself a hearty slap and wake up from that foggy nap! Gaze deep within where you will find precious love, sweet and sublime.

If you could be anybody that you wanted to be, would you still be you? Somebody's gotta do it, so it might as well be you.

Whenever I listen to spirit's voice, all is well.

Why search for love? It can never be found. It has always existed in God's light and sound.

Your creative imagination is the key to true spiritual liberation. Decide what you want in your life, and take the necessary steps to make it a reality. Listen to spirit's voice; heed it's subtle nudges, and allow love to be your guide.

Do you find yourself saying, "I can't take it any longer"? Well, simply stop taking it. Let it go, release it, and stop fighting yourself. Behold the love within your heart, and start "giving it." Ka-boom, baby!

Does the nasty old mind have you all flustered? Is it feeding you bowls of vile, rancid custard? Stop slurping that goop, and burp it all out. Replace it with love, and let your heart shout.

Chapter 15

Authority Figures

Once we discover love in our hearts, we stop seeking and asking questions because love is the only answer to which there is no question.

Eventually we discover that all truth and guidance come from within. Spiritual giants might inspire us, but in the end, we are the goddesses and gods of our own universe. We are all children of God. Let us love one another.

Life is about experience. Through countless lives, our minds are programmed with other people's ideas. Our peers, parents, education, religion, books, government, and culture inject us with their thoughts. We process them and call them ours. The only things we truly know arise from our personal experiences. Everything else is hearsay.

I was raised as a Catholic. From a very early age, I sensed something was awry. The teachings of the Church pointed their nasty finger of shame at me, saying that I was born with original sin because Adam and Eve had sinned. They warned that if I didn't get baptized, I would go to hell. Jesus, they claimed, had died for my sins two thousand years ago and I was indebted to God, as a result. Threats, guilt, repression, and fear—I moved on. looking for true love and found it in my heart.

Every time we tell someone to do things our way, we build walls around our heart, and our personal freedom is diminished.

If it weren't for followers, all leaders would be unemployed.

A conspirator is rendered powerless when he encounters a love-filled heart.

Are you feeling unruly today? Enjoy it. It means that no one can rule you.

Some belief systems state that humans were created in God's image. What I observe in today's world is that many people and organizations are attempting to reduce God to humanity's image for their own selfish motives. Does anybody want to buy some salvation? There seems be a lot of it for sale at bargain prices these days.

Myriad physical forms, philosophies, religions, art and scientific theories are born, have duration, and eventually pass away. Only love remains.

The only thing holding you back is you. Everything outside of you is beyond your control. Simply be who you are: magnificent, boundless, and beautiful. When I behold thy glory, I sing my thanks to God.

Enlightenment is not something that is discovered out there. No one can enlighten us. Others may inspire us, but ultimately, all truth comes from within. It begins with a discovery of one's true self, arising from a conscious desire to know the truth. Gaze into the splendor of your golden heart, and know that you are free.

If humanity abolished all religions, philosophies, and metaphysical systems of thought, they would simply pop up again in different manifestations. These mental creations arise from mass consciousness and are inevitable. The lower worlds are created in this fashion to temper humans.

An explorer crosses the Atlantic and discovers America. He bellows, "I found it!" His country of origin proclaims, "It belongs to us now." The natives are blind to the fact that they have been "discovered" and are about to be evicted from their ancestral home. This is how we came to be citizens of this country.

Many say that humanity is the apex of all creation. If this is true, I think it's time to revisit the drawing board.

Rather than saying "I beg to differ," stand up and stop begging: experience true spiritual freedom.

It's a natural human trait to project outward from our being and look for something to attach to: a hero, a book, a song, our job, our beliefs, etc. The outer world has the effect of taking our attention away from who we truly are: soul, child of God.

Some people think that they are majestic suns in a solar system around which all others should orbit; "legends in their own mind." The truth is we are all suns—gods and goddesses forever circling the gracious loving heart of God.

I'd never want to be a leader; leaders need followers. I choose to follow love's enchanting melody, forever singing in my heart, and gladly share it with you.

Wherever ego do you go?

Freedom is not something to be attained from someone else. All truth comes from within. The most a teacher can do is to guide another to their inner self. True love is a state of consciousness residing in your heart, waiting to be awakened and embraced.

Chapter 16

Here, There, Now, and Then

This is no journey's end. Love is all there is.

The only problem with "being here now" is that I'm always somewhere else when I'm thinking about it.

Truth is unwavering, yet in our world, it behaves like a chameleon, constantly changing its color, taste, aroma, and form to suit the mood and consciousness of the times.

Often, I wander through the worlds within my mind as a casual observer of the thoughts that blind my vision from the truth of who I am, of what I'm not, of where I've been, and why I've sought to go beyond this thought of my worldly existence.

"Be here now" is a famous spiritual axiom, but I don't buy into it. It sounds like the mind is telling me where and when to be. Buzz off, mind! I simply am, far beyond time, space, and every place.

"The stillness of the now?" More mind stuff. Stillness doesn't exist in time and space; activity is the law in the worlds of duality. One must rise above these planes to experience the stillness and the now.

Life is a spiritual process in which we gradually unfold. Enjoy being perfectly imperfect as you become who you are, drawing ever closer to your heart, love's true home.

Symbols are like catapults inspiring us to greater heights. Once their purpose has been served, we discard them. They can also be likened to windows or doors. We pass through them, move forward, and don't look back.

Rather than trying to access the "power of the now," release it from within your heart and enjoy love, power, and wisdom today. Why strive? You are the now! Freedom is already yours.

At the root of all things, behind all things, inside all things, outside of all things, and in the heart of all things rests the source of all things: divine love.

The greatest journey one can ever embark on is to consciously go nowhere at all.

My mind is a hurricane, and I am its eye. I have wings in my heart, and love is my cry!

The phrase "There's no time like now" is peculiar. From my perspective, it's "There's no time at all in now."

True spiritual freedom arrives when we have love, power, and wisdom all in balance.

All life is precious and is a gift from God; therefore, all life is worthy of respect and love.

Love is the answer to every question and problem in our lives.

Don't you just love being so perfectly imperfect? I do! It's a riot.

I love becoming who I am.

When we look outside of ourselves for answers to questions, we get trapped in a never-ending loop. Every answer leads to another question. Once we discover love in our hearts, we experience true spiritual freedom because love is the only answer to which there is no question.

I never try to make anyone feel welcome. I simply behold and acknowledge the "welcoming" residing in their hearts.

Sweet spirit, in your presence, I behold all the secrets left untold.

Are you basking in the glory of love's light? Feels awesome, eh? Now jump straight into its source, a golden sun shining in your heart.

Imagine yourself as an atom in a physical body. Pretty cool, eh? Now imagine that your body is an atom in a gigantic galaxy. Way cooler! You get the point—if you can imagine it, it already exists, so don't hold back. Walk beyond your self-imposed boundaries: imagine the very best in your life, and take the necessary steps to make it a reality.

If you aren't willing to consider the possibility of other worlds, higher planes, and inner states of consciousness beyond the mind, you will never discover them, let alone explore them. These other worlds exist in the moment, right now. Thou art a spiritual traveler, so venture forth into these remarkable worlds of love residing in your heart.

The answer to all of life's questions, perplexities, and challenges is singular and simple: we exist because of God's love. Love is the answer to every question. If we want love, we must give love; if we want freedom, we must grant others their freedom.

It is easy for the human mind to become fixated on symbols—powerful mental images packed with emotion. The mind creates these illusions to captivate our attention and prevent us from looking beyond them to the source of life itself. Divine love needs no symbol, intermediary or representative. It simply is and resides in every heart.

Symbols are majestic doors. As you pass through them, you release them and never look back.

Some of you may find this hard to believe, but you existed long before you were born.

Some modern day teachers describe the "now" as if it is something separate from and outside of us—something we have to seek, find, attain, or achieve. Forget these nebulous mental abstractions. You are the now.

Those who see action in inaction and inaction in action are looking through the mind's eye and have gained knowledge. Those who see spirit in its glorious splendor see only love with the spiritual eye and have attained wisdom.

Life is for living, and love is for giving. So what the heck are you waiting for?

Open the petals of your glorious heart, and let it all pour out. Shake those love atoms, sisters and brothers; make 'em twist and shout.

The difference between heart and mind is this: in the mind, everything is different; and in the heart, all is one.

I remember the very first time I consciously left my physical body. Since that time, I no longer fear death.

No distance in forever, in eternity no time: joyfully, I swim in thee, precious love sublime.

The circle has been a powerful symbol throughout human history. It is said to represent unity, completion, perfection, and God. As soul, I view circles as a limiting construct of the mechanical mind. I am free and live outside of all circles in the boundless ocean of spirit's love, where all circles have their being.

The distance between here, there, everywhere, and nowhere is infinite and infinitesimal.

I behold spirit's love in everyone and everything I see.

Living in the present moment, in the so-called now, means that everything you think, feel, and do carry very little wait.

Spirit is able to permeate all things. All it requires is a conscious soul. When a mother pours her love into a meal, this selfless act energizes the food, which enlivens her loved ones. Love is a gift from God that we share with others. Dip the ladle of love deep into your golden heart, sweet child of God, and pass it around.

When flames hold hands, a roaring fire is born.

Once you realize that you need nothing at all, then all will be yours.

Whenever you recognize and behold true love in the outer world, you are gazing into your heart.

Forget yesterday, forget tomorrow, and love now.

I prefer to be misbehaving with my heart than desperately craving in the murky haven of my mind.

> If I became you and you became me,
> Would we be each other?
> Would we be together?
> Would we have some fun?
> Would we have one heart?
> Would we be as one?

Don't be concerned with that well-known, much overstated "Be here now" spiritual axiom. I recommend "Being there later." I assure you, this philosophy is a real dandy! Forget about the moment and the now. There isn't enough time to think about it.

The largest circle the mind can possibly imagine sits within yet one more circle. Have you ever felt like you were going around in circles? I'm sure you can see where this is heading.

Chapter 17

Perfectly Imperfect

I know I am on the right path because all of this nonsense is starting to make sense.

As humans, we live in temporal bodies in a finite physical universe. Like it or not, all bodies pass away. So what are we left with except our true self? The best place for mind is back on the shelf.

One of the benefits of bringing out the worst in a person is that more room becomes available for the best.

"Now, now, now," said the present to the past, "you're a ship far out to sea, long gone without a mast."

Are you afraid of facing your fears, feeling disgraced, and drowning in tears? Does everything seem to be way out of place? Open your heart, accept spirit's grace, and surround yourself with a loving embrace.

God believes in me, so how can I possibly be an atheist?

Limitations are nothing more than self-imposed ghostly misconceptions. They vaporize into thin air when you learn to see through the walls, but first, you have to see the walls.

We never attain a state of complete perfection where we proclaim, "I finally made it!" Only God is perfect. There is always one more step. We can always do better, act more kindly, and radiate more love. Spirit shines through conscious souls to light up the worlds.

Repeatedly making the same mistake is one of the few instances in which the more we succeed, the greater our failures.

I love being so perfectly imperfect because it means there's a whole lotta room for improvement. Bring on the goods!

Each life is a step as we return again and again. We move ever forward, gaining experiences along the way, always drawing nearer to the simple truth behind all life; we exist because of God's love.

Do you have trouble accepting a sincere compliment or a loving gift? Do you feel you must give something back? We have been programmed to react this way by tradition, religion, education, government, peers, etc. When a gift is given in love, there is no expectation from the giver and no debt is incurred. Being able to accept a gift graciously is an important lesson some of us have to learn.

Change arises from within each individual and is reflected in the world without.

Is there anything more wondrous, delicious, and entertaining than an imperfect human being trying to describe perfection?

The only difference between you and me is that we aren't the same.

As human, we tend to look outside of ourselves and take it all in. I have a suggestion. How about gazing into our hearts first, and then putting it all out?

I'm far beyond reason and right out of my mind. I can't imagine having a better time.

Five hundred lifetimes immersed in worlds of music; composers, musicians, singers, and songs are everywhere. You soak in the richness of these worlds life after life, imbibing countless experiences into the memory of your being. In your 501st lifetime, you are born with amazing natural musical talents. The world marvels at your genius. You are an amazing soul, the sum of your life's experiences.

The expression "You only live once" is hilarious. To one, it means "Do as much as I can while I can." To another, it means "Take as much as I can while I can." As soul, I do live once, and it's forever. Every day, I shine a little brighter on my journey back home.

All of us are learning and growing right now, in this instant, as we speak, as we listen. Enjoy being perfectly imperfect as you discover who you are.

What is difficult for one is easy for another. We have unique experiences with different lessons to learn and progress at our own pace. Awareness of this is how we develop patience, respect, and compassion for others and ourselves.

Imagination is a wonderful spiritual gift we all possess. For some reason, in the human state of consciousness, people find it easier to imagine a lot of negative stuff. I know because I am human too. Once we look into our hearts and discover love residing within, we begin to see it in others and in the world around us.

Before enlightenment: wake up, feed the kids, do the dishes, go to work, walk the dog, watch Oprah, log in to Facebook, etc. After enlightenment: wake up, feed the kids, do the dishes, go to work, walk the dog, watch Oprah, log in to Facebook, etc.

Who invented this planet anyway? Believe it or not, we did. Life on earth as we know it is an expression of humanity's combined thoughts, feelings, and actions. Instead of trying to change the world, we should strive to discover our true nature; soul, child of God, perfect and free. As we unfold, the world will appear differently.

Often, karma acts swiftly; we get a boot in the butt and know exactly why something is happening to us. At other times, it takes years; and having forgotten our past actions, we say, "Why is this happening to me? What did I do to deserve this?' We reap what we sow. Karma works in its own time, and the ledger always gets balanced. There's no escaping responsibility.

This morning, I awoke feeling extremely insecure. So precarious was my condition that upon seeing my face in the mirror, I immediately demanded three pieces of photo ID to make sure that it was truly I. Speaking from my own experience, I can assure you that it is perfectly OK to be negative and harbor doubts once in awhile.

Whenever you think that something is impossible, it simply means that you haven't considered all the possibilities.

The way we see the world is determined by our inner states of consciousness. When we change, the world appears differently.

Life is a process of gaining self-awareness, and there is no set formula. As individuals, we learn in unique ways at our own pace. Once we realize that all life exists because of God's love, we begin to open like a flower smiling at the sun.

Why flatter an ego? It's much too big for its size. Scoop warm love from your heart, and drip some into its eyes.

Unending cycles of temporary pleasure and gratification is all that the outer world can offer. Peace and joy lie forever waiting within your golden heart. If you hug yourself sincerely and in the right place, a rainbow sun will explode in your eyes and set you free.

Forget playing with the double-edged laws of attraction, playthings of the mind, which keep you fixated on things of the outer world. Everything you need, you already have. Love glows forever in your heart and is its own reward.

I would rather be a container than the things that I contain. That's why I use my heart to love instead of thinking with my brain.

Anytime something appears hopeless, you are viewing it through the myopic eye of the mind. Your heart sees only love.

When searching for truth, there shouldn't be anything underlying anything. If there is, keep on digging until you find nothing.

The difference between psychic power and spiritual power is this: the psychic attempts to manipulate and direct the dual-natured forces of nature for specific purposes. Psychic energy is the temptation of mind. Spiritual power flows from God into the hearts of loving souls and serves only to uplift humankind.

Come to think of it—the more I think about it, the less it makes sense. But then again, the less I think about it, the more sense it seems to make.

I don't subscribe to the idea of karma because it calls for too much personal responsibility.

Hey mind, stop feeding me crumbs and vinegary wine. Go stick your head where the sun doesn't shine.

If you find yourself trying to be different, then you are behaving like most people. You are incredibly unique and special. Relax, sweet soul, and be yourself. You rawk!

Chapter 18

Kindness

Extending our noble thoughts, warm feelings, and acts of loving kindness to others is like offering a magic carpet ride. Love elevates their hearts, enlivens their senses, and liberates them from the shackles of their minds while reflecting back to us the love we have shared.

The giving of love is a spiritual expression of the greatest significance.

Your acts of kindness are iridescent wings of divine love, which linger and continue to uplift others long after your sharing.

Instead of looking for differences and peculiarities, embrace the loving similarities.

I've never felt such fingertips like the ones inside my heart; the softness of your loving touch blows my mind apart.

I will never try to make you happy. I can clearly see the joy in you, and I love to coax it out because when you laugh, my heart cries with delight.

A little known spiritual approach is to do our best to extend goodwill to all living beings and give warm love only to those who return it. The result is a cycle of creative energy, which attracts like-minded and like-hearted souls.

To be fortunate or blessed means that we have earned a spiritual gift called grace—arising from our noble thoughts, loving feelings, and acts of kindness.

When we look for the best in others, it is surprising what we find: how well they respond to love and leave their woes behind.

Whoops! I didn't mean to spill my love all over you. Actually, I did it on purpose. Feel free to immerse yourself completely in the sublime liquid and soak it all in. Only good can come of it.

I have so much love to share that I carry two large buckets, one in each hand to catch some of the overflow constantly spilling from my heart. I could use some help. Wanna lighten my load a little?

We can always tell if something has truly been well said, because it is usually well heard.

As individual children of God, we are composed of the same spiritual atoms, but we express ourselves uniquely. Bring it on, set it loose, and let 'er rip! Life is for living, and love is for giving, so give it all you've got.

As soul, you are a magnificent spiritual prism. The singular, pure love light of God enters your open heart and is distributed to others by the grace of your noble thoughts, loving feelings, and acts of kindness.

Chapter 19

Letting Go

Congratulations! I heard that you lost your mind. Don't waste your time looking for it. Enjoy your newfound freedom.

Egg? Larva? Cocoon? Embryo? Spirit's liberating light and sound beckons. Bust loose, spread your magnificent wings, and soar the infinite spiritual skies of love deep within your golden heart. Feels good, eh?

A question cannot exist without its opposite: an answer. Every answer leads to another question. Round and round and round she goes. One way to rise above the worlds of the dual-natured mind is to stop asking questions.

> Have you ever gazed upon a star as it zooms across the sky,
> Shining in its splendor and screaming its love cry?
> Have you ever wondered what life is, what God is, and who you are?
> Life is love, love is God, and you are that wondrous star.

Are you tired of being a second-rate actor in someone else's B movie? Trash that scene, and create your own Oscar-worthy feature film. Produce it, direct it, and give yourself the leading role. Go for it! It's your life, and it must be worth living, or you wouldn't be here. Write yourself a juicy script pulsing with adventure, power, love, and freedom.

Attachment has nothing to do with our possessions. Attachment is about what possesses us.

Hey! How long have you been pulling that wagon? What? You didn't even realize it was there? Simply let go. It's that easy.

At the exact moment I stopped searching for truth, it found me.

Are you attached to the idea of becoming detached? There is nothing to detach from, and there is nothing to know. This concept originates in the mind, which is a very poor master. Simply let go, gaze into your heart, and behold the splendor of God's infinite love.

> Take off those goggles that boggle your mind,
> Rip off those glasses that render you blind.
> Open your heart, and there you will find an
> ocean of love, sweet and sublime.

My veils disappear when your love passes through me. My atoms ring, and my grateful heart sings, "You are my everything."

The more we let go, the more we have. The things we hang on to don't belong to us. Let go of what you don't have, and set yourself free!

Tenacity strangles the love in your heart. When you are relaxed, secure in spirit's embrace, love is able to flow freely from your heart and permeate the very essence of life. Release your grip; there is nothing to hold on to. You are love, sweet soul. Set thyself free.

Surrender is letting go of our fears, expanding our awareness, and opening up to God's divine love. The act of surrendering is a liberating force through which we receive the bounty of spirit's grace.

The word "worry" derives its meaning from Middle English *worien*, from Old English *wyrgan*, and is akin to old High German *wurgen*—"to strangle"—and Lithuanian *verzti*—"to constrict." When we worry, we cut off love's flow, denying ourselves spirit's grace. I once met a woman who said to me,

"Don't tell me worrying doesn't work because I worry all the time, and nothing ever happens to me."

Instead of getting even or teaching someone a lesson when they do you wrong, consider teaching yourself a lesson instead. Revenge keeps you psychically connected to another in a negative way. Release yourself through the liberating act of forgiveness, and learn a truly valuable spiritual lesson.

Trying to be perfect is a waste of time. Why carry a bucket when you're swimming in the ocean?

> What's this you say—my own wings I must spread?
> Fly my own vision beyond my small head?
> But my wings are quite rusty, and it's been oh-so-long
> since I've taken to flight and followed your song.
> Oh, now I remember; the dream is returning.
> Love's sweet voice in my heart, it's the truth I am yearning.

Bored, timid, or lazy? Feeling disgruntled? How about an adventure? Consider doing something out of the ordinary; live a little on the razor's edge. Take a chance, try something you consider risky, and step out of your comfort zone. Trust your spiritual nature, and let your imagination carry you away. You have nothing to lose and so much to discover.

Do your thoughts and feelings have you stumbling and reeling? Do you crash down to the floor and reverb off the ceiling? If you open up your heart, true love will surely follow: say goodbye forever more to cold, dark, and hollow.

Once you realize that there is nowhere to go, you have finally arrived.

Why fear the future when there is only the now?

In your heart burns a mystic fire, always growing and reaching higher. Allow its flames to set you free.

Lust, anger, attachment, vanity, and greed are links in an insidious chain that keep many enslaved. Mind is the padlock binding you to this chain, and the key to opening it lies within your heart.

Are you trying to break free of things that don't exist? Barriers are merely ghostly apparitions of the mind. Immerse yourself in the boundless ocean of divine love residing in your golden heart, and set yourself free.

Living your life through the eyes of the ego is like worshipping your reflection in a mirror. Why keep the cowardly mind happy? Grab a lightning bolt from your heart, and smash that mirror to bits. Now what do you see?

The problem with expectations is that you are focused on the future instead of the ever-present moment of the now.

One way to get more out of life is to stop thinking about death.

Look in the mirror, and walk through your fear. Wake up in your heart, and see your love clear.

A negative thought is like a runaway train on a one-track mind, whilst a loving soul gently lifts the hearts of humankind.

Love is the electricity in your heart, which powers the mechanical mind. Simply press the off button, and discover your true self as soul—resplendent, perfect child of God.

Hardship or heart ship? You choose the ride. You can wallow in darkness or embrace love inside.

Every time I leave my physical body, I am no longer concerned about having to be "some" body. I love being "no" body, a state in which I am "every" body.

Chapter 20

Soul—Your True Self

If you use the expressions "my soul" and "your soul," you have yet to discover your true nature. Soul is not a thing that you possess. You *are* soul.

Don't try to fit me into anything,
There is no such container.
I am soul, and I am free,
It's simply a no-brainer.

A finely tuned mind under the guidance of soul is like a sacred slingshot. It can fling us up to the lofty worlds of divine love and is then discarded, for it has served its purpose.

Eventually, we discover our true nature as resplendent souls and realize that since time immemorial, mind has been casting swine at pearls.

Consider this. You are not your body, your feelings, or your thoughts. You are soul, eternal and perfect, captain of your mystic ship. gods and goddesses of your universe. Set your sails, and allow the winds of loving spirit to fill your golden heart and carry you away.

Stop choosing, and become the chosen one. Divine love awaits thee, precious soul.

Thou art resplendent soul: a shining beacon of God's limitless and indomitable love. I behold thee and celebrate your true spiritual nature. Love thyself, sweet child of God, and allow the brilliance of your golden heart to shine forth.

Soul, in its self-realized state, is like a wild stallion: noble, free-spirited, unfettered, and spontaneous, forever roaming the wondrous skies of heaven. Humans without spiritual awareness are like tamed workhorses: corralled, kept in reign by the mind, and forever following the dictates of others.

I occupy no space whatsoever. I'm everywhere yet can't be found. I am spirit's loving light and sound.

All souls are connected through the indomitable love of spirit.

Volunteers are grateful souls who pass on to others the love that spirit has graciously bestowed upon them.

Are you wandering around in a body, thinking you have a soul? No wonder life is so tough. You *are* soul using a sentient body as an instrument of perception, expression, and experience in the physical worlds. Believe it or not, your body is like an overcoat. Uncover your heart, and enjoy a newfound freedom that has always been yours. Bodies die, but you live forever.

The optimist sees the donut, the pessimist the hole. I see shimmering rays of love in the heart of every soul.

Your physical, emotional, and mental bodies are protective devices, which cover soul, your true resplendent self. You wear them as instruments of perception and expression while gaining experience in the lower worlds.

A human being without spiritual wisdom is the seeker, looking everywhere in the fleeting worlds of time and space, the worlds of the mind. Soul is the knower gazing inwardly and thriving in the ever-present moment of the now.

Beholding our true radiant self for the first time is like watching a phoenix rising from the ashes.

Forget all that DNA stuff. You *are* soul, and you *have* a body. Whenever you meet someone, look beyond their body and behold soul, a unique spiritual entity.

There is a deep longing within each soul to return to its true home from whence it came.

Where love shines, darkness cannot exist. Every soul is a light unto itself.

Soul in its natural state is neither male nor female. It is a pure individualized atom of God's love.

I looked down at my light body. Billions of sparkling, dancing atoms pulsed and glowed with an effervescence that left me breathless. A multitude of colors, textures, and shapes cascaded and intermingled in a celebration of love. I experienced life with higher senses and felt a joy I had never known before. I am soul; free and complete within myself.

In our spiritual journey, we eventually discover an enormous power behind all life. Many choose to tap into it and use it for their own purposes. A humble soul is one who has access to all of this power, moves beyond it, and chooses love. Soul is spirit's brilliant beacon of love, power, and wisdom.

The further we are from divine love, the more attached we become to our ideas and possessions, forgetting our spiritual nature as soul. If someone insults me, criticizes my lifestyle, or questions my spiritual points of view, I don't get fazed. I am soul, just like you: child of god, perfect and free.

I look for love in the hearts of everyone I meet.

Love thyself as soul, not as a person. People vanish and bodies die. Love is an eternal beacon residing in your heart. Shine on, and fear nothing. Look beyond your body and rejoice as you behold spirit's resplendent light and sound within.

Divine truth manifests over and over again and is expressed by conscious souls.

I love the child of wonder within all of us; perfect soul, sparkling effervescence of God's limitless love.

I am a scintillating atom of spirit's divine love, forever beating in your heart.

Whenever you touch me, an ancient phoenix slowly rises from the ashes deep within my heart. I am reborn and rise far beyond the heavens of religion into the golden vestibule of life. I am soul and sunbathe forever in the warmth of your indomitable love.

As soul, I'm too wrapped up in the glorious adventures of the ever-present moment to worry about past lives and future events such as dying and prophecies.

Exquisite spiritual butterfly, art thou! Open your golden heart and set thyself free! Spread wide thy glistening wings: soar high above heaven's sky. You are resplendent soul: eternal, perfect, and brimming with divine love.

As spirit's love fills me, the more individualized and free I become as I realize my purpose as soul.

An inspired soul is one through which spirit's love flows like a glorious river of light and an ecstatic song of joy. The sublime sweetness of spirit's holy breath always brightens, enlivens, and enriches every heart.

You can't conspire against a soul whose heart pulses with a spiritual fire.

Awesome art thou, sweet shining soul: a magnificent tree of life reaching high into the heavens. Your every leaf shimmers like a golden sun, your sweet summer smile breathing love into the heart of life.

A soul does not develop. It is enveloped by many coverings. and unfolds like origami, releasing God's loving light and sound from its spiritual heart, love's true home.

I'm not a saint, guru, master, or redeemer. I am soul, dream's eternal lover and love's eternal dreamer.

Are you looking out for yourself, your loved ones, and your best interests? Try looking in. Your heart is a shimmering reservoir of divine love. Once you recognize your exquisite spiritual nature and behold yourself as soul, the outer world will appear differently: you will see love everywhere.

We have a human side and a spiritual side. Many believe they are a body, seek to satisfy its cravings, worry about death, and rely on the approval of others to give meaning to their lives. Soul views the body as an instrument of perception, expression, and experience—destined to perish. Our true self sees divine love and is oblivious to the tasteless crumbs of illusion offered up by the mechanical mind.

Each soul has a unique spiritual color, flavor, texture, and aroma. Open your heart, and allow spirit's sweet love to flow.

Invisible strands of love, light, and sound connect all souls.

Can you help me? No, thanks. I'm way beyond help. I am soul, and I am free.

I don't know how else to say it. I am soul. I always see love when I look into your hearts.

I am the soft feathers of your wings, bright constellations in your skies, and a flame of love flickering in your astonishing eyes.

Anytime I experience a bout of spiritual heartburn, I reach for my precious bottle of Soulaids (not to be confused with Rolaids) for instant relief.

I'm a bratty little devil with a crumpled halo tucked into the back pocket of my faded blue jeans. I love poking my pitchfork at the mind, and with my heart, I love all humankind.

Love is a river flowing from God into our hearts. As it flows out again to all life, it takes a little bit of our unique flavor with it. We are vehicles for spirit, God's love. This is the very essence of life. We exist because of God's love; we are all children of God. Can it get any simpler?

We all carry the seeds of love. Reach into your glowing heart and embrace the sparkling gem of spirit's light and sound. Behold the love, wisdom and power, which have always been yours. Plant these precious seeds into the fertile gardens of your divine imagination; nurture them with the sweet essence of your resplendent self. Thou art soul, child of God, perfect and free.

There is no such thing as one big behind-the-scenes objective reality. Everyone has his or her own unique reality, and we are entitled to our points of view. An awareness of this creates respect for others. If someone says they can lead you to reality, chances are they are referring to their reality. As soul, you choose your experiences and create your own reality.

In the heart of every being shines a golden sun.

Chapter 21

The Heart of the Matter

As soon as I realized that I was a boomerang of love, I turned around and started heading straight for your heart, love's true home.

I speak to the spiritual heart, not the human heart. The heart of soul is the conduit for God's love.

Only one act is worth repeating: love.

If you feel uncomfortable when someone extends you a sincere compliment, it means your mind is getting in the way. Open wide the precious petals of your love, and accept it wholeheartedly.

In one sense, there is nothing to discover, except perhaps within your heart where you'll find the perfect lover.

There are many different ways to look at humans. I look beyond the face and behold the sweet grace glowing in each and every heart.

Living a spiritual life is not about doing without or living in austerity and denial. It's about doing within. In the heart of every being shines a golden sun. Behold yours, and celebrate! You truly are something special. Shine on!

If you think frolicking and surfing on love's waves is an awesome experience, imagine what it would be like to dive deep into the splendor of its glorious liquid heart and soar high above its jewel-filled sky.

Those who truly point the way have their finger aimed squarely at your heart. Love thyself as I love thee, precious friend.

I stand drenched under the waterfall of your perfect love. Wash over me, Great Spirit: carry me to my true home in the bosom of your loving heart.

I am a grain of love pollen floating on the warm breeze within your sacred heart.

When I say that I would like to turn you on, I am referring to the love light in your heart.

Embrace yourself so hard that you squeeze the love right out of your heart. Eventually, you will learn to let it flow in a more gentle fashion.

No matter how lost you may feel, no matter how forlorn or deep your despair, gaze into your heart, my love, for I am always there.

I am a sea of tranquility, and as the fragrant rose petals from your golden heart gently fall upon me, waves of divine love radiate outward and uplift all God's children.

My heart is an exploding supernova! I love you and all life.

Are you experiencing an uplifting tingling sensation deep within your heart? Surprise! It's me! I'm dancing and frolicking atop the shimmering waves in the ocean of your love.

The only vessel capable of forever quenching every hunger and thirst is your golden heart overflowing with divine love.

My radiant heart sprouts two lovely golden wings; and off I go, fluttering and singing as I scatter luminescent sparks of love dust, light beams, and celestial sounds every which way. I'm sharing God's love. Want some?

Out of your mind and into your heart—the very best way for soul to start its journey back home.

I've been looking for a long, long time for this
thing called love.
I've ridden comets across the sky, and I've
looked below and above.
Then one day I looked inside myself, and this is
what I found:
A golden sun residing there, beaming forth
God's light and sound.

Wow! I just peered inside my heart, and there you were, so
I thought I would drop in for a friendly visit and give you a
gigantic hug.

Your heart is a poem in love's true home.

In the center of a serene, majestic ocean, I sat next to my
master in a tiny boat. "How vast and beautiful it is," I
gasped in wonder. Smiling with sparkling benevolent eyes,
he whispered gently, "The ocean you behold is merely the
surface of your precious heart. Immerse yourself into its
glorious depths, sweet soul, and discover your spiritual
nature. You are the splendor of God's divine love."

Gradually, we learn to trust spirit; and as we do, our hearts
open like a flower smiling at the sun.

Within the deepest chamber of every heart glows an
inextinguishable flame of divine love.

My eyes always twinkle with joy when they gaze upon spirit's
beautiful face smiling in your heart.

O glorious sun within my heart, the light of you is all I see;
your rays of love escape my chest and forever set me free.

By opening our hearts, we draw closer to the worlds of Spirit. Our creative imagination is the key. Imagine only the very best in your life, and then take the necessary steps to make it a reality.

Embrace the love within your heart, and behold it in others.

A push from the outside is not what is required; a nudge from within you is the key. Listen to love's gentle whispers in your heart.

Recognizing divine love in our hearts takes us beyond the mind—beyond worry, doubt, suspicion, anger, greed, vanity, attachment, and fear.

Imagine your heart as a glorious, tranquil, infinite ocean. When Holy Spirit drops a single pebble of love into its center, waves of divine inspiration radiate outward and uplift all life.

My love-filled heart soars through your sky; my tears form rainbows as I cry.

Joy is not a stranger you meet along the way. Joy is your best friend and passionate lover living in your heart each and every day.

If something appears to be totally "pointless," it's because you're aiming with your mind instead of gazing within your heart.

When spirit's light and sound radiate from a loving heart, the human voice is capable of becoming the most exquisite, refined, and divine musical instrument.

The on/off switch for the mechanical mind is smack dab in the center of your loving heart.

Do your senses rule you, or do your senses guide you? If you are uncertain, listen to the heart inside you.

The mind hunts like a vulture, the heart flutters like a dove. I choose to be a free bird and soar the skies above.

You may have heard the expression "We are what we think." My experience has been that "I am what I don't think." The mind is a wonderful servant but a very poor master, always complicating the simplest matters by drawing our attention to things in the outer world. It's time for a lovely swan dive out of my mind and straight into my heart.

I am nestled in your every heartbeat and with you throughout each day.

Anything that has an opposite doesn't truly exist. Physical things all pass away and are nothing more than wispy apparitions offered up by the mind to keep you fixated on things of the outer world. There is no opposite to divine love—the source of your being—glowing and pulsing in the center of your golden heart.

I am a mischievous rapscallion and love being who I am. I don't claim to be perfect by any means. I'm on a quest for love and know exactly where to find it. Do you mind if I open the door to your sweet, luscious heart? It's cold and dark out here.

Chapter 22

You Rawk!

Gosh! There's so much love overflowing from the ocean in your heart that I have to wear hip waders whilst I walk your blessed shores.

Your very existence is living proof that God has bestowed upon you the highest seal of approval, so don't worry about what others think of you. You rawk!

Did you know that at the beginning and end of every glorious rainbow rests your loving heart?

> Have you ever gazed upon a star as it zooms across the sky, shining in its splendor and screaming its love cry?
> Have you ever wondered what life is, what God is, and who you are?
> Life is love, love is God, and you are that wondrous star.

If only you could see yourself the way I see you: billions of stars illuminate your eyes; undulating waves of liquid love beckoning to me from the ocean deep within your heart.

You're the best at being you that I have ever seen: so kiss yourself right on the lips, you gorgeous human being.

In this world of too many "wise guys," it is a supreme joy to meet a truly resplendent "wise geyser." Love gushes out of you and washes away all my fears.

Surprise! The way we see ourselves is not the same way others see us. We all rawk!

I think that most of us see what we want to see, expect to see, and what we have been told to see. When I gaze into the eyes and hearts of my brothers and sisters, I see love. What do you see?

I've never loved eyes so deep,
I drown in them and give to sleep.
I stir, I rise, and I rejoice; I'm home at last!
With spirit's voice, my heart beats fast.

I never laugh at a person. I do chuckle at the imagery being evoked at any given moment by a person's thoughts, feelings, and actions. Let's face it: we humans are a hoot! Of course, I say this in a loving manner.

You're anticipating the liftoff as the seconds tick away. What the heck are you waiting for? Blast off! Now! Today!

Attention everyone! Wanna see something incredibly stunning, alluring, sexy, smart, smoldering hot, irresistibly gorgeous, and overflowing with goodness and intelligence? Walk over to the nearest mirror and look straight into it. Surprise! Aren't you something special? I know you are, so give yourself a gigantic hug.

I would never consider being someone else. My plate's too full of being me.

The hand of God lifted me up and dropped me gently into the warm waters of your inimitable love.

I love waking up in the bosom of your heart. There's no better way for life to start.

We are soft feathers of iridescent gold-winged hearts soaring the wondrous skies of spirit's divine love.

When your love embraces me, I melt into your heart and flow back into myself.

I'm a ravenous tiger, and I'm hot on your scent. I roam the jungle paths, and upon your heart, I'm bent.

Your sweet moonbeams gently stir my cup and whip my cream.

> Eyes of wonder,
> Eyes of light,
> Eyes of spiritual beauty, bright.

Long before McDonald's was on the scene, I was already lovin' it: life, that is, and especially you.

I have never met anyone who excels at being you the way you do. You are so good at it: you totally rawk!

Life is for living, and love is for giving so give it all you've got.

A flock of alabaster doves erupts from my heart, and I smile as the soft feathers of your love alight upon the glowing hearts of your precious children below.

I enjoy playing in the wonderland of your heart.

> I can't possibly go too far, you're much too profound.
> You're higher than my sky and deeper than my ground.
> There seems to be no end in you as my love spins round and round,
> So I melt into your heart and drink your light and sound.

I find it easy to love you. As I embrace myself, your love flows like a river from my heart.

I love to fly high above the tenderness of your glowing heart. A gentle breeze lifts me to invisible worlds, distant and deep.

I am a joy-filled firefly as I sprinkle the shimmering atoms of your love into the exhilarating eyes of life.

The most effective way of learning how to love others is to love you first.

Drowning deep within you is the only way to go: when my mind stops breathing, your sweet love starts to flow.

The part of you that the physical eyes can't see is the one that I find to be outstanding.

If life weren't worth living, you wouldn't be alive right now.

The sweet intoxicating scent of you enlivens all my senses. My walls collapse with no more fences as I say goodbye to all pretenses.

Instead of trying to make the most out of life, allow life to make the most out of you. Everything you could possibly require resides in your heart, so give it all you've got because love is all there is.

You are infinitesimally enormous. That was very big of you in a tiny sort of way.

> Your sweet breath stirs the pond in my ponder.
> Your starlit eyes invoke the wand in my wander.
> I yearn to wander in your pond, far beyond,
> forever gone: deep within your precious heart.

The silver-tipped waves of your sweet love lake make me wanna bake a birthday cake.

Chapter 23

Facebook Love

Facebook is a living expression of humans using language in a creative fashion. Words conjure up images brimming with emotions; and on the Internet, our words, thoughts, and feelings transcend time and space, allowing us to share with each other. It's magical, and it's spiritual. Let us smile, shine, and share spirit's love today.

Spirit's love flows into me like a mighty river. I marvel as thoughts, emotions, and images cascade out of my mind and splash into my heart like a waterfall, where they dance, frolic, and mingle in a frothy bliss. The next thing I know, inspirational thoughts, humor, prose, and poems of divine love emerge as waves upon this river as it flows onto the pages of Facebook and into the hearts of my loving friends.

I thank all of my Facebook friends for the wonderful insights they share with me every day. I bask and grow in the inspirational glow of God's love shining from each of your golden hearts.

Every time I am able to tear asunder my surreptitious mind, blessed arrows of sweet inspiration burst from my heart and alight ever so gently onto the pages of Facebook. OK, sometimes they crash with a boom.

Many use Facebook because of a desire to connect and share. When I gaze into the eyes and hearts of my Facebook friends, I see love. What are you sharing today?

Facebook is a remarkable living, breathing novel emoting the wonders and diversity of the incredible human spirit. Each one of us is a living page in this mesmerizing tale. Don't you just love our enchanting story as it continually unfolds?

Imagine this. We are all in deep space, aboard the US starship *Facebook*, searching for signs of intelligent life, and come upon planet Earth. Abiding by the sacred law of noninterference, we only observe. What conclusions might you come up with regarding the state of humanity on planet Earth?

The amazing spirit of God permeates and transcends the fabric of life and uses whatever loving instruments are available so it can uplift, inspire, and heal. Spirit is working its magic right now as it connects loving souls via Facebook.

I hope everyone is enjoying this fine day because I stayed up all night making it. I am exhausted, but my loving Facebook friends are well worth the effort.

Facebook is a mirror for me. When I look at you, I love what I see.

I am soul, an individual spark of God's inimitable love, just like you. Spirit nudges me to write, and when I listen to my Facebook friends with an open heart, I am a cup. Love fills me up until it spills out onto the pages of Facebook and becomes a shimmering river flowing into the hearts of others.

When I connect with my Facebook friends, I paint a picture on the canvas of their minds and offer it as a gift of love. My heart is spirit's brush evoking mystic landscapes in your imagination. I am a whimsical soul, a child in so many ways. I love to share and play with you.

Love is not something that we do. Love is what we are. We exist because of God's love. An awareness and appreciation of this truth has changed my life completely. When I look at and listen to my Facebook friends, I behold love in their hearts.

The sweetness of your love drips all over my Facebook pages.

Facebook sure is pulsing with wonderful waves of liquid love this fine day. Woo-hoo! Bring it on baby! I am singing.

Whenever spirit tickles me, humor flows out of my heart and onto the pages of Facebook. I hoot and holler, jump and laugh as spirit's love uplifts my friends.

Chapter 24

Sweet Tweets for Soul

If you don't give it all you've got, it won't be got and will soon be forgotten: all for naught, withered, and rotten.

The heart of soul is the conduit for God's love.

When I say that I would like to turn you on, I am referring to the love light in your heart.

Within the deepest chamber of every spiritual heart glows an inextinguishable flame of divine love.

You are a divine package of effervescent love containing the sun, the prism, and the rainbow.

You've got quite a life, I like the way you live it. I like the way you laugh, and I love the way you give it.

We are soft feathers of iridescent gold-winged hearts soaring the wondrous skies of Spirit's divine worlds.

Gaze into your heart where mind has no power and love reigns supreme.

Making a conscious choice to enter or exit a circle is much different than unwittingly living inside someone else's circle.

When everyone is insane, no one notices.

You're the best at being you that I have ever seen, so kiss yourself right on the lips, you gorgeous human being.

There's nowhere to go, so what's your hurry?

Being half asleep and half awake is not one and the same.

If it weren't for the fact that I see things differently, I would probably agree with you.

I rely on nothing because I have everything.

From divine love is born wisdom, power, and freedom.

The farther you can see, the less you have to look.

True love can never be measured: it can only be treasured.

Your words so smooth, your passion so strong, you could talk a nightingale out of its song.

As more loving souls light up, the brighter life becomes.

One way to get more out of life is to stop thinking about death.

Love is a gift from God that we share with others.

Love is the prime creative force. How well we work with it determines the nature and quality of our experiences.

One way to escape the confines of the mind is to let go of what we don't have.

God believes in me, so how can I possibly be an atheist?

I learn from myself 'cause there's nobody else.

Mind is the padlock binding you to the chains of illusion: the key to opening it lies within your heart.

Only humans try to live and love; microorganisms, plants, and animals mastered it billions of years ago.

After studying polygamy for several years, I concluded that there are too many sides to consider.

I am your kite without a string; you are my everything.

The rays of your sweet love light nourish, invigorate, and purify me.

When we look for the best in life and express ourselves in a loving fashion, our words can work wonders.

All knowledge is a few dollars short of wisdom, which lies in your heart, love's true home.

The mechanical mind out of control has a singular goal: to show you the pieces and make hidden the whole.

You are the thunder in my wings and the lightning in my eyes: your love's the only fuel I need to fly these friendly skies.

Every time we praise the mind, we are worshipping a machine.

Mind is only a machine, but somehow, it has become the ultimate weapon of mass seduction.

Billions of shimmering stars illuminate your mysterious eyes; undulating waves of liquid love beckon me from the ocean deep within your heart.

I like what you do and the way that you do it; you never get down, and you never say screw it.

I only live once, and as soul, child of God, it's forever.

Pull your viewpoint way back, further than you've ever been, and you will see that love is everywhere.

We are souls, eternal and perfect, captains of our mystic ships: gods and goddesses of our universe.

I'm a kid. I love it, and I don't wanna grow up. I'm not a snarly old hound; I'm a happy young pup.

You are soul: not a body or your feelings, not your thoughts or your mind.

I look beyond the face and behold the sweet grace shining in each and every heart.

A true hero acts from a loving heart, without regard for self, and sacrifices all for another.

Why flicker like a flame when a roaring fire burns inside?

I just realized that I have spent my entire life getting to where I am right now.

Look in the mirror, and walk through your fear; wake up in your heart, and see your love clear.

Grab a tennis racket, and give your fear a real good whack: send that sucker so far off it's never coming back.

My wings flutter in anticipation of your arrival, sweet woman.

Learning to accept a gift graciously is an important lesson some of us have to learn.

We can always shine brighter, act more kindly, and radiate more love.

Spirit constantly seeks more beacons to shine its love light.

We all have unique experiences, with different lessons to learn, and we progress at our own pace.

Karma works in its own time, and the ledger always gets balanced; there's no escaping responsibility.

Love begets love and is the only law.

Drowning deep within you is the only way to go.

Once we realize that we exist because of God's love, we open like a flower smiling at the sun.

> Don't be afraid of living,
> No reason to fear death.
> You're much more than a body,
> Inside lies untold wealth.

If I became you and you became me, would we be as one, and would we be free? Would you lend your credit card to me?

Whenever you meet someone, look beyond their body and behold soul, a unique spiritual entity.

My mind is a machine; my heart is electricity. When you push my buttons, we become sweet synchronicity.

Rise above mental ideas, and discover who you truly are by expressing yourself fully from the heart.

Allowing oneself to be worshipped and put on a pedestal creates an illusion that one is better than others, guaranteeing a swift, hard fall.

Heroism seeks no fame and is love in action.

Only by surfing the cosmic waves in the ocean of your loving heart are you able to transcend life's problems and discover your true spiritual nature.

If a teacher, guru, or instructor acts as if he or she knows it all, chances are they know very little.

When a gift is given in love, no debt is incurred.

A good teacher inspires through example, not just flowery words, sparkling eyes, and animated gestures.

An aura is but one manifestation of your true self: why study a flashlight when the sun shines above?

Since all matter eventually disintegrates, science is incapable of knowing anything of any lasting value.

You are the now; freedom is already yours, so why strive for anything?

Love glows forever in every heart and is its own reward.

Symbols are majestic doors. You pass through them and never look back.

How happy you are, and so you should be; from that glint in your eye, I can tell you are free.

No distance in forever; in eternity, no time. Joyfully, I swim in thee, precious love sublime.

You know where you've been, and you know where you're going, 'cause you live from the heart and your love's always flowing.

Love is a gift from God that we share with others.

Love is the answer to every question.

Itsy-bitsy morsels for the puny little mind: chunks of lies to nibble on until the end of time.

Your heart is a living, breathing canvas for spirit's light and sound, capable of inspiring and uplifting others.

Allowing others to express their points of view is called respect.

Take your frown, and flip it upside down; now you have a smile, so share it for a while.

I woke up this morning with a smile upon my face; I perceived the beauty and felt the warm grace of your love.

I am a grain of sand upon your beach of love; your gentle breath doth lift me up to my true home above.

Intuition beckons from beyond the mind, bringing opportunity, joy, and bounty into our lives.

There isn't much point in being a bird if you don't spread your wings and fly.

These things I imagine are the things that I like, so I take them with me when I'm riding my bike.

Your imagination is a divine instrument that can set you free.

Many people pursue goals that others have deemed worthwhile.

Why strive for love when it sits waiting in your heart?

Every time we wrap ourselves around each other, our spiritual atoms intermingle in an effervescent dance of joy!

In my heart, I have a tummy; and when you dive in, it whispers, "Yummy."

I love being a beach on the shoreline of your love.

Your warm iridescent waters beckon me with every wave as you pull me from the sand: I'm a sandman flowing through your hands.

Love is the only answer to which there is no question.

Once you realize that there is nowhere to go, you have finally arrived.

Instead of trying to learn a new skill, let it learn you by expanding your consciousness and allowing it to grow.

I never stop and never start; I am spirit's love, which fills your heart.

Enjoy being perfectly imperfect as you become who you are.

The fear of nothing is the greatest of all fears.

Whenever you perceive a problem, remember that every answer rests in your loving heart.

Being lighthearted is a key to happiness.

All souls exist because of God's Love.

The incessant mechanical mind strives to keep soul's attention fixated on things of the outer world lest it discover divine love glowing in its heart.

Life after life, we inhabit various forms: mineral, plant, insect, bird, mammal, and human. Eventually, we discover our true nature as soul.

Jump up and down, and make lots of noise; that's what I expect from good girls and boys.

A symbol is a distraction erected by the mind to prevent you from moving beyond, into endless worlds of love forever beating in your heart.

There is life on other planets: only the ego of man would consider itself to be the apex of all creation.

Catapult yourself high above the confines of the mind: pull yourself back further than you've ever been, and you will see that love is all there is.

Words such as size, distance, before, and after are meaningless to the heart.

Experience is the only true teacher.

Imagine the very best in your life, and take the necessary steps to make it a reality.

In today's technologically advanced societies, there isn't a single scientific instrument capable of measuring love.

Only one thing can travel faster than the speed of light: a carload of shoppers heading for Boxing Day specials at Wal-Mart.

Within the empty space that many refer to as "nothing" exist innumerable worlds of wonder teeming with life and filled with divine love.

Gratitude opens up our hearts to the gifts of spirit.

I have just overdosed from a massive injection of divine love: there's no cure, and fortunately, it's highly contagious.

Mind, a much greater force than gravity, keeps our consciousness trapped in the lower worlds of time and space.

I'm a solitary tiger roaming the sultry tropical forest of your heart: I never tire on my journey as I draw closer to the fountain of your love.

A fact for sure is nothing true; it's just a single point of view.

Some say this, and some say that; but you know where loves at, and because of that, you're a real kewl cat.

If something is explained in complex terms, it is usually very distant from truth.

I am forever infected with sweet love radiating from your immaculate, contagious smile.

Getting a driver's license is a memorable experience; every time I get mine back, I celebrate.

Rather than trying to access the power of the now, release it from within.

Every sparkling atom of my being soaks in your sweet love.

As soul, I'm too wrapped up with the glorious adventures in the ever-present moment of the now to worry about past lives and future events.

> Row, row, row your boat gently down the stream,
> Deep within your golden heart, where love has always been.

Look beyond human bodies, and rejoice as you behold spirit's resplendent light and sound within every heart.

Whenever you touch me, an ancient phoenix slowly rises from the ashes deep within my heart.

Symbols are erected by the mind to prevent you from moving beyond, into the eternal worlds of love residing in your heart, love's true home.

When you sing your song of love, I am reborn and rise far beyond the heavens of religion into the golden vestibule of life.

You spin madly like a cyclone across my wild terrain as you stir the love within my heart, and annihilate my brain.

Anyone can criticize; I prefer to spark your eyes and lift your heart to golden skies.

Soul is like a wild stallion: noble, free-spirited, unfettered, and spontaneous—forever roaming the wondrous skies of heaven.

Open wide thy golden heart, exquisite butterfly, and set thyself free!

I'm really glad that you are you and so happy I am me; let's jump off this magic cloud and dive into the sea.

Since love is all there is, there are no such things as opposites.

Where there's a will, there's a way, while a horde of lawyers and greedy relatives fidget, bicker, and drool on the sidelines.

Ladders are useful devices for those who have yet to discover their wings.

I have nothing to give because I am all yours, sweet spirit.

Living in the present moment, in the now, means that everything we think, feel, and do carry very little wait.

The sweetest of all things is love from the heart.

Liquid smiles pour from your eyes and lift my heart to golden skies.

A loving heart flows like a resplendent waterfall into the hearts of others: for those who are willing, it just keeps on filling.

If you want to see something truly spectacular, replace everything with nothing, and all shall be revealed.

Sometimes I'm crashing, thrashing, and bashing along; whatever I'm doin', my passion is strong.

If you hug yourself sincerely and in the right place, a rainbow sun will explode in your eyes and set your free.

It is easier to dig a tunnel to the center of the earth with a toothpick than it is to find divine love with the mind.

When it comes to duality, there are two sides to every story.

Just because it feels good doesn't mean it's good for you.

The reason that you love the way I write is because I write the way you love.

I love being so perfectly imperfect because it means there's a whole lotta room for improvement.

Your heart is a poem in love's true home.

Repeating the same mistake over and over again is one of the few instances where the more you succeed, the more difficult life becomes.

I love to fly high above the tenderness of your glowing heart; a gentle breeze lifts me to invisible worlds, distant and deep.

Your loving heart is love's true home: it's where you live and shine.

Constantly changing my routine is part of my daily routine; life never gets boring.

I am a flame, reaching higher and higher as I breathe in the heat of your intense desire.

As soul, we gradually unfold like origami, releasing God's loving light and sound from our hearts, love's true home.

Each beat of your glowing heart gives birth to brilliant constellations.

Your glorious love light shatters my mind into a million fragments and sets me free.

You are love: nothing more need be said in the ever-present moment of the now.

When we judge someone, we are attempting to extinguish the spiritual essence of that being and our personal freedom is diminished.

In today's world, democracy means the freedom to get away with as much as you can without getting caught.

A true spiritual creation of a high magnitude is made manifest when soul allows spirit's love to enter and flow through its heart.

Borders are ghostly apparitions of the mechanical mind.

Immerse yourself into the center of your golden heart, and set yourself free.

If you're feeling unruly today, enjoy it: it means that no one can rule you.

The mind is literally terrified to death of nothing, because within nothing lies everything.

If something appears to be totally "pointless," it's because you're aiming with your mind instead of gazing within your heart.

Recognizing divine love in our hearts takes us beyond the mind—beyond worry, doubt, suspicion, anger, greed, vanity, attachment, and fear.

When you live a life full of love, your heart radiates sparkling atoms of truth, which serve to uplift all mankind and set you free.

I feel like Rumi on a rocket, zooming through the heavens with your warm heart in my pocket.

If something appears to be unreasonable, you are most likely heading toward your heart, love's true home.

Allow spirit's heavenly breath to fill the sails of your heart ship.

The symptoms of a very serious "staff" infection is when everyone in the office is complaining and gossiping.

Once you realize that you need nothing, all will be yours.

It's amazing what we can do with love and even more amazing what love can do with us.

The sweet perfume of thy simmering love permeates my grateful heart: you truly are heaven's scent.

How lovely it is to drown in your waters and be reborn as a wave of liquid love dancing upon the surface of your golden heart.

Your love makes a lot of scents, and my grateful heart inhales them all.

Love is totally out of my control, and I thank God for that.

I'm the crust, and you are the topping; your hot tangy sauce has my love atoms popping!

I don't think I could possibly love you more: I know I can always love you better.

I no longer face my fears; they were blinded by your love and fell into arrears.

I'm joyful when our atoms merge into a loving molecule; the way our passion clusters, I think it's really kewl.

We whirl around each other as sparks fly everywhere; colliding with such tenderness, there's nothing to compare.

I am a troubadour sitting upon the window ledge of your heart.

Within every event and inside every atom, there is an infinite amount of space brimming with divine love.

Your heart is all shiny, sparkly, and bright; your eyes, constellations bringing joy to the night.

I didn't think I could get any higher 'til my heart dove into the depths of your fire.

Your smile streaming comets, your hair liquid fire—woman, thou art my heart's one desire.

My love-filled heart soars through your sky; my tears form rainbows as I cry.

The farther we can see, the less we have to look.

Mind without a heart is like gas without a fart: the pressure keeps building, and there's no relief in sight.

I wasn't reading your mind. It was reading me.

Many people believe they are what they eat. I prefer to eat what I am.

I am a little honeybee laden with pollen. I can taste your sweet nectar; I can hear your heart callin'.

The only problem with being here now is that I'm always somewhere else when I'm thinking about it.

Mind can't comprehend the concept of nothing because it imagines itself to be a big, wonderful, and irreplaceable something.

Whenever you think that something is impossible, it simply means that you haven't considered all the possibilities.

Sweet love, skip my heart across the ocean like a stone; I'm coming home!

A loving heart leaves a beautiful mark without intending any gain, while a selfish mind has endless goals and always leaves a stain.

The harder you look, the less you will find; so trust in your heart and abandon the mind.

The light of you is all I see: with darkness gone, now I am free.

Human beings are living proof that God has an incredible sense of humor.

If it weren't for followers, all leaders would be unemployed.

Wrap yourself around me, woman, until my love erupts. A honeybee my heart is now, and you my buttercup.

When your love embraces me, I melt into your heart and flow back into myself.

Whoever invented the phrase "I'm bored" probably had nothing better to do.

Whoops! I apologize, Mr. Mind; I didn't mean to kick you between the thoughts.

The ego is wrapped up with itself in constant adulation: a frantic, self-indulgent, repugnant mindsturbation.

Rather than saying "I beg to differ," stand up, stop begging, and experience spiritual freedom.

Woman, you are my heart's only desire and transform my flame into a raging fire.

I didn't realize I was sleeping until I woke up (to the truth).

I am not on a mission: I am love's mission.

Life after life, we return, gaining experience along the way, drawing nearer to the truth that we exist because of God's love.

I fly far beyond every known sky and soak up the warmth of your generous smile.

I hover in the light of your radiant eyes, then abandon my wings, and dive into your fire.

Whenever you giggle, tiny love bubbles burst out of your heart and sprinkle upon me like golden rain-shine.

My tears of joy are transformed into glittering emeralds when they alight upon your love-filled heart.

I love taking a bubble bath in the fountain of your heart.

Mind is blind, and love sees all.

All I can say about pleasure and joy is "I'm glad you're a girl, and thank God I'm a boy."

I know it is unethical—theft is not allowed. But I just want to steal your heart 'cause it melts away my shroud.

Never judge a cover by its book.

The love I feel for life is so overwhelming that tears of joy and gratitude stream out of my eyes, glide down my chest, and drip into my heart.

The most insidious prison is one in which the inmates think they are free.

Such joy I experienced this morning when I woke up and discovered that I still had a pulse.

I would rather be a moron than a moroff.

If life weren't worth living, you wouldn't be alive right now.

Life could be likened to a sandwich: everyone wants a bite, but not everybody wants to share.

My insanity is the only thing preventing me from losing my mind!

A recent survey suggests that pregnancy is a leading cause of childbirth.

The human desire to be included stems from a mind that is self-deluded.

I didn't realize what all the laughter was about until I looked in the mirror.

Luscious love drips from your lips and seeps into my heart; it stirs an ancient longing and blows my mind apart.

Infants are the root cause of all senior citizens.

Geez! If this keeps up, it will never come down.

Your acts of kindness continue to uplift others long after your sharing.

How wonderful it is to watch as you sleep and awaken in my own dream, entwined with you as we make love in one of God's glorious paintings.

I love the way you compliment yourself when you tell me how wonderful I am.

I was born in Synchroni City, but somehow, I ended up in Tena City.

When we see beauty within ourselves, our hearts become like suns, radiating love to everyone we encounter on our journey back home.

The things that can't be proven by the logical mind are truths beyond all space and time.

It is so quiet in here that I can hear a mouse peeing on a Kleenex.

If we don't like what we see, we are the ones who have to change.

The only thing I don't like about being a child is that everybody wants me to grow up.

Thou art the candle, and I am the flame; I burn forever in thy name.

If you don't like your job, it means you're not doing what you should be doing.

Freedom can't be found and love can't be attained: both lie waiting in your heart, far beyond your brain.

Did you know that whenever you compliment someone in a sincere fashion, you are stirring the love pudding in his or her heart?

Love cures all.

You and I are the perfect loving equation.

The optimist sees the donut, the pessimist the hole: I see shimmering rays of love in the heart of every soul.

The most effective way of learning how to love others is to love you first.

There's no limit on dreams, and your heart is boundless, so what the heck are you waiting for?

If you're gonna do it, then just do it: nothing will ever get done if you just say, "Screw it."

Allowing another person to express their point of view is a vital step in our personal spiritual development.

Your existence is living proof that God has bestowed upon you the highest seal of approval.

My former psychic was shocked and surprised when I dropped in unexpectedly.

A person whom a dimwit considers to be brilliant is nothing more than a slightly brighter dimwit.

I am nestled in your every heartbeat and with you throughout each day.

The fact that greed can be shared is an oxymoron of immense proportions.

"Now, now, now," said the present to the past, "you're a ship far out to sea, long gone without a mast."

Soul is enveloped by many coverings: it unfolds like origami, releasing God's loving light and sound from its precious heart, love's true home.

Why does spontaneity always show up unexpectedly?

I welcome your opinion as long as you don't make any suggestions.

The bigger I get, the smaller it seems; when I crumple my fear, I wake up in my dreams.

A person who is forever Jung is in fact an ancient being.

Trying to be perfect is a waste of time: why carry a bucket when you're swimming in the ocean?

It's a long way to nowhere; and the last time I arrived, I didn't realize I was there until long after I had departed.

Did you know that at the beginning and end of every glorious rainbow rests your loving heart?

I love to kiss your tender skin; my heart melts when you let me in.

The fact that you can perceive a problem is proof that you can solve it.

I can taste your sparkling pheromones as they wander through my mist; they land upon my love-filled heart with a luscious juicy kiss.

The distance between here, there, everywhere, and nowhere is infinite and infinitesimal.

Spread your wings and fly so high, straight through the sun into a brand new sky.

The only difference between an atom and a solar system is size.

If my love gets any higher, I'll have to pull out my divine excavator and start digging for heaven.

Every smile and twinkle in your eyes is a new chapter forever enchanting my heart.

If you hold a circle in your hands and give it a half twist, it becomes the symbol for infinity.

When we smile, our eyes sparkle with an effervescence and warmth, which endears us to and uplifts those around us.

Whenever your incandescent smile gently whispers its fragrant breath, the flickering flame within my heart bursts into a roaring fire.

At home or office, at work or play, share your smile with someone today.

You don't wake up from a true dream; you wake up in it.

Whenever we experience fortune or grace in our lives, God's light and sound is smiling upon us.

A symbol might seem awesome at first, until you realize that it stands between you and the real thing.

Divine love has no reason, needs no reason, and is far beyond reason.

The problem with letting go is that it leaves me with nothing to hang on to.

An eye for an eye and a tooth for tooth leaves everyone blind and feeling uncouth.

Don't even think about being someone else.

Thought after thought, mile after mile, I love to watch the space between my thoughts where spirit waits with a loving smile.

Every time I lose my mind, I find myself dwelling in the magical worlds of light and sound within my heart, love's true home.

My radiant heart sprouts two lovely golden wings, and off I go, scattering specks of love dust and celestial sounds every which way.

I love intermingling with you; our heart song, a love jingle as our senses tingle from the invigorating warmth of Spirit's holy breath.

Looking down on others is bad karma unless, of course, they are shorter than you.

Joy is your best friend and passionate lover living in your heart each and every day.

Whenever someone makes us smile, pleases us, and inspires us, we are enjoying a reflection of ourselves—full of love, beauty, goodness, and grace.

An inspired soul is one through which spirit's love flows like a glorious river of light and an ecstatic song of joy.

It's cold and dark out here: do you mind if I open the door to your sweet, luscious, and lovely heart?

The sublime sweetness of spirit's holy breath enriches every heart.

I ended up being me because no one else wanted the job.

Have you ever stopped and listened to love's permeating sound, the celestial music of the spheres that all the saints have found?

Hand in hand, we walk along the shores of life; whitecaps foam and whisper tales, then disappear again.

We are gods and goddesses of our own universe.

Spirit is the giver, and we are the rivers through which love flows.

The words I breathe are spirit's love infused with the unique essence of my true self.

In your heart burns a mystic fire, always growing and reaching higher.

No teaching is worth a pinch of mouse poop unless it is imbued with divine love and speaks to the heart

A negative thought is like a runaway train on a one-track mind, whilst a loving soul gently lifts the hearts of all mankind.

If someone is driving you mad, just hop off the bus, and soon, you'll be glad.

I am a happy little honeybee, merrily buzzing along as I sprinkle crystals of love's sweet nectar into the heart of every flower I meet.

Your exquisite beauty turns me on like a radio, my grateful heart broadcasting spirit's message of sweet love to all who will listen.

Sharing the same flame is a fun game to play with you as trumpets sing our names from the heavens high above.

Your scorching beauty and intoxicating aroma makes my heart pop like a cosmic lollipop.

Upon inner reflection, I reach a love connection intersection, which lifts me to your sweet perfection.

Sweet nectar lies within thee, precious woman, and flows like a majestic waterfall from your heart into mine.

Although love has no real words, a gentle heart and noble mind can imbue words with a spark that awakens divine love within others.

I can't wait to find out how old I'm going to be when I grow up.

Dear Mr. Opinion and Ms. Bad Advice: You're not a brush in my hair. You're more like head lice.

Many who predict the future or look into the past don't have a clue what's going on right now.

There's gotta be a way to make this nanosecond last longer. Whooosh! Oh well, here comes another one.

If it's true that we only use 10 percent of our brains, can you imagine the ensuing madness if the remaining 90 percent suddenly hopped on the bandwagon?

> I breathe you in, you breathe me out and new
> worlds are created,
> The gentle touch of your sweet love, my heart
> forever sated.

Made in the USA
Lexington, KY
07 February 2011